THE IMITATION OF
CHRIST

THE IMITATION OF CHRIST

DOVER THRIFT EDITIONS

Thomas à Kempis

Translated by
Aloysius Croft and Harold Bolton

DOVER PUBLICATIONS, INC.
MINEOLA, NEW YORK

DOVER THRIFT EDITIONS

GENERAL EDITOR: PAUL NEGRI
EDITOR OF THIS VOLUME: SUSAN L. RATTINER

Bibliographical Note

This Dover edition, first published in 2003, is an unabridged republication of *The Imitation of Christ*, translated from the Latin by Aloysius Croft and Harold Bolton, as published by the Bruce Publishing Company, Milwaukee, Wisconsin, in 1940.

Library of Congress Cataloging-in-Publication Data

Imitatio Christi. English.
   The imitation of Christ / Thomas à Kempis ; translated by Aloysius Croft and Harold Bolton.
      p. cm. — (Dover thrift editions)
   Originally published: Milwaukee : Bruce Pub., 1940.
   ISBN-13: 978-0-486-43185-7 (pbk.)
   ISBN-10: 0-486-43185-1 (pbk.)
      1. Meditations. I. Thomas, à Kempis, 1380–1471. II. Croft, Aloysius. III. Bolton, Harold. IV. Title. V. Series.

BV4821.K44 2003
242—dc21   2003051559

Manufactured in the United States by LSC Communications
43185113   2020
www.doverpublications.com

Foreword

IN PREPARING this edition of *The Imitation of Christ*, the aim was to achieve a simple, readable text which would ring true to those who are already lovers of this incomparable book and would attract others to it. For this reason we have attempted to render the text into English as it is spoken today rather than the cloudy, archaic terminology that encumbers so many translations of Christian classics. The result, we feel, has achieved a directness and conciseness which will meet the approval of modern readers. In the second place, we have made use of the familiar paragraph form, doing away with the simple statement or verse form of the original and of many translations. This was done in the interest of easier reading, and in order to bring out more clearly the connection between the single statements.

No claim of literary excellence over the many English versions now extant is here advanced, nor any attempt to solve in further confusion the problem of the book's authorship.

Theories most popular at the moment ascribe the *Imitation* to two or three men, members of the Brethren of the Common Life, an association of priests organized in the Netherlands in the latter half of the fourteenth century. That Thomas Hemerken of Kempen, or Thomas à Kempis as he is now known, later translated a composite of their writings, essentially a spiritual diary, from the original Netherlandish into Latin is generally admitted by scholars. This Thomas, born about the year 1380, was educated by the Brethren of the Common Life, was moved to join their community, and was ordained priest. His career thereafter was devoted to practicing the counsels of spiritual perfection and to copying books for the schools. From both pursuits evolved *The*

Imitation of Christ. As editor and translator he was not without faults, but thanks to him the *Imitation* became and has remained, after the Bible, the most widely read book in the world. It is his edition that is here rendered into English, without deletion of chapters or parts of them because doubts exist as to their authorship, or because of variants in style, or for any of the other more or less valid reasons.

There is but one major change. The treatise on Holy Communion, which À Kempis places as Book Three, is here titled Book Four. The move makes the order of the whole more logical and agrees with the thought of most editors.

THE TRANSLATORS
Aloysius Croft
Harold Bolton ·

Contents

BOOK ONE

THOUGHTS HELPFUL IN THE
LIFE OF THE SOUL

BOOK FOUR
AN INVITATION TO HOLY COMMUNION

BOOK ONE

THOUGHTS HELPFUL IN THE LIFE OF THE SOUL

The First Chapter

IMITATING CHRIST AND DESPISING ALL VANITIES ON EARTH

HE WHO follows Me, walks not in darkness," says the Lord.[1] By these words of Christ we are advised to imitate His life and habits, if we wish to be truly enlightened and free from all blindness of heart. Let our chief effort, therefore, be to study the life of Jesus Christ.

The teaching of Christ is more excellent than all the advice of the saints, and he who has His spirit will find in it a hidden strength. Now, there are many who hear the Gospel often but care little for it because they have not the spirit of Christ. Yet whoever wishes to understand fully the words of Christ must try to pattern his whole life on that of Christ.

What good does it do to speak learnedly about the Trinity if, lacking humility, you displease the Trinity? Indeed it is not learning that makes a man holy and just, but a virtuous life makes him pleasing to God. I would rather feel contrition than know how to define it. For what would it profit us to know the whole Bible by heart and the principles of all the philosophers if we live without grace and the love of God? Vanity of vanities and all is vanity, except to love God and serve Him alone.

---

[1] John 8:12.

1

This is the greatest wisdom—to seek the kingdom of heaven through contempt of the world. It is vanity, therefore, to seek and trust in riches that perish. It is vanity also to court honor and to be puffed up with pride. It is vanity to follow the lusts of the body and to desire things for which severe punishment later must come. It is vanity to wish for long life and to care little about a well-spent life. It is vanity to be concerned with the present only and not to make provision for things to come. It is vanity to love what passes quickly and not to look ahead where eternal joy abides.

Often recall the proverb: "The eye is not satisfied with seeing nor the ear filled with hearing."[2] Try, moreover, to turn your heart from the love of things visible and bring yourself to things invisible. For they who follow their own evil passions stain their consciences and lose the grace of God.

The Second Chapter

HAVING A HUMBLE OPINION OF SELF

EVERY MAN naturally desires knowledge; but what good is knowledge without fear of God? Indeed a humble rustic who serves God is better than a proud intellectual who neglects his soul to study the course of the stars. He who knows himself well becomes mean in his own eyes and is not happy when praised by men.

If I knew all things in the world and had not charity, what would it profit me before God Who will judge me by my deeds?

Shun too great a desire for knowledge, for in it there is much fretting and delusion. Intellectuals like to appear learned and to be called wise. Yet there are many things the knowledge of which does little or no good to the soul, and he who concerns himself about other things than those which lead to salvation is very unwise.

Many words do not satisfy the soul; but a good life eases the mind and a clean conscience inspires great trust in God.

The more you know and the better you understand, the more severely will you be judged, unless your life is also the more holy. Do not be proud, therefore, because of your learning or skill. Rather, fear because of the talent given you. If you think you know many things and understand them well enough, realize at the same time that there is much you do not know. Hence, do not affect wisdom, but admit your

---

[2] Eccles. 1:8.

ignorance. Why prefer yourself to anyone else when many are more learned, more cultured than you?

If you wish to learn and appreciate something worth while, then love to be unknown and considered as nothing. Truly to know and despise self is the best and most perfect counsel. To think of oneself as nothing, and always to think well and highly of others is the best and most perfect wisdom. Wherefore, if you see another sin openly or commit a serious crime, do not consider yourself better, for you do not know how long you can remain good. All men are frail, but you must admit that none is more frail than yourself.

The Third Chapter

THE DOCTRINE OF TRUTH

HAPPY IS he to whom truth manifests itself, not in signs and words that fade, but as it actually is. Our opinions, our senses often deceive us and we discern very little.

What good is much discussion of involved and obscure matters when our ignorance of them will not be held against us on Judgment Day? Neglect of things which are profitable and necessary and undue concern with those which are irrelevant and harmful, are great folly.

We have eyes and do not see.

What, therefore, have we to do with questions of philosophy? He to whom the Eternal Word speaks is free from theorizing. For from this Word are all things and of Him all things speak—the Beginning Who also speaks to us. Without this Word no man understands or judges aright. He to whom it becomes everything, who traces all things to it and who sees all things in it, may ease his heart and remain at peace with God.

O God, You Who are the truth, make me one with You in love everlasting. I am often wearied by the many things I hear and read, but in You is all that I long for. Let the learned be still, let all creatures be silent before You; do You alone speak to me.

The more recollected a man is, and the more simple of heart he becomes, the easier he understands sublime things, for he receives the light of knowledge from above. The pure, simple, and steadfast spirit is not distracted by many labors, for he does them all for the honor of God. And since he enjoys interior peace he seeks no selfish end in anything. What, indeed, gives more trouble and affliction than uncontrolled desires of the heart?

A good and devout man arranges in his mind the things he has to do,

not according to the whims of evil inclination but according to the dic-
tates of right reason. Who is forced to struggle more than he who tries
to master himself? This ought to be our purpose, then: to conquer self,
to become stronger each day, to advance in virtue.

Every perfection in this life has some imperfection mixed with it and
no learning of ours is without some darkness. Humble knowledge of
self is a surer path to God than the ardent pursuit of learning. Not that
learning is to be considered evil, or knowledge, which is good in itself
and so ordained by God; but a clean conscience and virtuous life ought
always to be preferred. Many often err and accomplish little or nothing
because they try to become learned rather than to live well.

If men used as much care in uprooting vices and implanting virtues as
they do in discussing problems, there would not be so much evil and scandal in the world, or such laxity in religious organizations. On the day of
judgment, surely, we shall not be asked what we have read but what we
have done; not how well we have spoken but how well we have lived.

Tell me, where now are all the masters and teachers whom you knew
so well in life and who were famous for their learning? Others have
already taken their places and I know not whether they ever think of
their predecessors. During life they seemed to be something; now they
are seldom remembered. How quickly the glory of the world passes
away! If only their lives had kept pace with their learning, then their
study and reading would have been worth while.

How many there are who perish because of vain worldly knowledge
and too little care for serving God. They became vain in their own conceits because they chose to be great rather than humble.

He is truly great who has great charity. He is truly great who is little
in his own eyes and makes nothing of the highest honor. He is truly
wise who looks upon all earthly things as folly that he may gain Christ.
He who does God's will and renounces his own is truly very learned.

The Fourth Chapter

PRUDENCE IN ACTION

DO NOT yield to every impulse and suggestion but consider things carefully and patiently in the light of God's will. For very often, sad to say, we
are so weak that we believe and speak evil of others rather than good.
Perfect men, however, do not readily believe every talebearer, because they
know that human frailty is prone to evil and is likely to appear in speech.

Not to act rashly or to cling obstinately to one's opinion, not to believe everything people say or to spread abroad the gossip one has heard, is great wisdom.

Take counsel with a wise and conscientious man. Seek the advice of your betters in preference to following your own inclinations.

A good life makes a man wise according to God and gives him experience in many things, for the more humble he is and the more subject to God, the wiser and the more at peace he will be in all things.

The Fifth Chapter

READING THE HOLY SCRIPTURE

TRUTH, NOT eloquence, is to be sought in reading the Holy Scriptures; and every part must be read in the spirit in which it was written. For in the Scriptures we ought to seek profit rather than polished diction.

Likewise we ought to read simple and devout books as willingly as learned and profound ones. We ought not to be swayed by the authority of the writer, whether he be a great literary light or an insignificant person, but by the love of simple truth. We ought not to ask who is speaking, but mark what is said. Men pass away, but the truth of the Lord remains forever. God speaks to us in many ways without regard for persons.

Our curiosity often impedes our reading of the Scriptures, when we wish to understand and mull over what we ought simply to read and pass by.

If you would profit from it, therefore, read with humility, simplicity, and faith, and never seek a reputation for being learned. Seek willingly and listen attentively to the words of the saints; do not be displeased with the sayings of the ancients, for they were not made without purpose.

The Sixth Chapter

UNBRIDLED AFFECTIONS

WHEN A man desires a thing too much, he at once becomes ill at ease. A proud and avaricious man never rests, whereas he who is poor and humble of heart lives in a world of peace. An unmortified man is quickly tempted and overcome in small, trifling evils; his spirit is weak, in a measure carnal and inclined to sensual things; he can hardly abstain from earthly desires. Hence it makes him sad to forego them; he is quick to anger if reproved. Yet if he satisfies his desires, remorse of conscience overwhelms him because he followed his passions and they did not lead to the peace he sought.

True peace of heart, then, is found in resisting passions, not in satisfying them. There is no peace in the carnal man, in the man given to vain attractions, but there is peace in the fervent and spiritual man.

The Seventh Chapter

AVOIDING FALSE HOPE AND PRIDE

VAIN IS the man who puts his trust in men, in created things.

Do not be ashamed to serve others for the love of Jesus Christ and to seem poor in this world. Do not be self-sufficient but place your trust in God. Do what lies in your power and God will aid your good will. Put no trust in your own learning nor in the cunning of any man, but rather in the grace of God Who helps the humble and humbles the proud.

If you have wealth, do not glory in it, nor in friends because they are powerful, but in God Who gives all things and Who desires above all to give Himself. Do not boast of personal stature or of physical beauty, qualities which are marred and destroyed by a little sickness. Do not take pride in your talent or ability, lest you displease God to Whom belongs all the natural gifts that you have.

Do not think yourself better than others lest, perhaps, you be accounted worse before God Who knows what is in man. Do not take pride in your good deeds, for God's judgments differ from those of men and what pleases them often displeases Him. If there is good in you, see more good in others, so that you may remain humble. It does no harm to esteem yourself less than anyone else, but it is very harmful to think yourself better than even one. The humble live in continuous peace, while in the hearts of the proud are envy and frequent anger.

The Eighth Chapter

SHUNNING OVER-FAMILIARITY

DO NOT open your heart to every man, but discuss your affairs with one who is wise and who fears God. Do not keep company with young people and strangers. Do not fawn upon the rich, and do not be fond of mingling with the great. Associate with the humble and the simple, with the devout and virtuous, and with them speak of edifying things. Be not intimate with any woman, but generally commend all good women to God. Seek only the intimacy of God and of His angels, and avoid the notice of men.

We ought to have charity for all men but familiarity with all is not expedient. Sometimes it happens that a person enjoys a good reputation among those who do not know him, but at the same time is held in slight regard by those who do. Frequently we think we are pleasing others by our presence and we begin rather to displease them by the faults they find in us.

The Ninth Chapter

OBEDIENCE AND SUBJECTION

IT IS a very great thing to obey, to live under a superior and not to be one's own master, for it is much safer to be subject than it is to command. Many live in obedience more from necessity than from love. Such become discontented and dejected on the slightest pretext; they will never gain peace of mind unless they subject themselves whole-heartedly for the love of God.

Go where you may, you will find no rest except in humble obedience to the rule of authority. Dreams of happiness expected from change and different places have deceived many.

Everyone, it is true, wishes to do as he pleases and is attracted to those who agree with him. But if God be among us, we must at times give up our opinions for the blessings of peace.

Furthermore, who is so wise that he can have full knowledge of everything? Do not trust too much in your own opinions, but be willing to listen to those of others. If, though your own be good, you accept another's opinion for love of God, you will gain much more merit; for I have often heard that it is safer to listen to advice and take it than to give it. It may happen, too, that while one's own opinion may be good, refusal to agree with others when reason and occasion demand it, is a sign of pride and obstinacy.

The Tenth Chapter

AVOIDING IDLE TALK

SHUN THE gossip of men as much as possible, for discussion of worldly affairs, even though sincere, is a great distraction inasmuch as we are quickly ensnared and captivated by vanity.

Many a time I wish that I had held my peace and had not associated with men. Why, indeed, do we converse and gossip among ourselves when we so seldom part without a troubled conscience? We do so because we seek comfort from one another's conversation and wish to ease the mind wearied by diverse thoughts. Hence, we talk and think quite fondly of things we like very much or of things we dislike intensely. But, sad to say, we often talk vainly and to no purpose; for this external pleasure effectively bars inward and divine consolation.

Therefore we must watch and pray lest time pass idly.

When the right and opportune moment comes for speaking, say something that will edify.

Bad habits and indifference to spiritual progress do much to remove the guard from the tongue. Devout conversation on spiritual matters, on the contrary, is a great aid to spiritual progress, especially when persons of the same mind and spirit associate together in God.

The Eleventh Chapter

ACQUIRING PEACE AND ZEAL
FOR PERFECTION

WE SHOULD enjoy much peace if we did not concern ourselves with what others say and do, for these are no concern of ours. How can a man who meddles in affairs not his own, who seeks strange distractions, and who is little or seldom inwardly recollected, live long in peace?

Blessed are the simple of heart for they shall enjoy peace in abundance.

Why were some of the saints so perfect and so given to contemplation? Because they tried to mortify entirely in themselves all earthly desires, and thus they were able to attach themselves to God with all their heart and freely to concentrate their innermost thoughts.

We are too occupied with our own whims and fancies, too taken up with passing things. Rarely do we completely conquer even one vice, and we are not inflamed with the desire to improve ourselves day by day; hence, we remain cold and indifferent. If we mortified our bodies perfectly and allowed no distractions to enter our minds, we could appreciate divine things and experience something of heavenly contemplation.

The greatest obstacle, indeed, the only obstacle, is that we are not free from passions and lusts, that we do not try to follow the perfect way of the saints. Thus when we encounter some slight difficulty, we are too easily dejected and turn to human consolations. If we tried, however, to stand as brave men in battle, the help of the Lord from heaven would surely sustain us. For He Who gives us the opportunity of fighting for victory, is ready to help those who carry on and trust in His grace.

If we let our progress in religious life depend on the observance of its externals alone, our devotion will quickly come to an end. Let us, then, lay the ax to the root that we may be freed from our passions and thus have peace of mind.

If we were to uproot only one vice each year, we should soon become perfect. The contrary, however, is often the case—we feel that we were better and purer in the first fervor of our conversion than we are after many years in the practice of our faith. Our fervor and progress ought to increase day by day; yet it is now considered noteworthy if a man can retain even a part of his first fervor.

If we did a little violence to ourselves at the start, we should afterwards be able to do all things with ease and joy. It is hard to break old habits, but harder still to go against our will.

If you do not overcome small, trifling things, how will you overcome the more difficult? Resist temptations in the beginning, and unlearn the evil habit lest perhaps, little by little, it lead to a more evil one.

If you but consider what peace a good life will bring to yourself and what joy it will give to others, I think you will be more concerned about your spiritual progress.

The Twelfth Chapter

THE VALUE OF ADVERSITY

IT IS good for us to have trials and troubles at times, for they often remind us that we are on probation and ought not to hope in any worldly thing. It is good for us sometimes to suffer contradiction, to be misjudged by men even though we do well and mean well. These things help us to be humble and shield us from vainglory. When to all outward appearances men give us no credit, when they do not think well of us, then we are more inclined to seek God Who sees our hearts. Therefore, a man ought to root himself so firmly in God that he will not need the consolations of men.

When a man of good will is afflicted, tempted, and tormented by evil thoughts, he realizes clearly that his greatest need is God, without Whom he can do no good. Saddened by his miseries and sufferings, he laments and prays. He wearies of living longer and wishes for death that he might be dissolved and be with Christ. Then he understands fully that perfect security and complete peace cannot be found on earth.

The Thirteenth Chapter

RESISTING TEMPTATION

SO LONG as we live in this world we cannot escape suffering and temptation. Whence it is written in Job: "The life of man upon earth is a warfare."[1] Everyone, therefore, must guard against temptation and must watch in prayer lest the devil, who never sleeps but goes about seeking whom he may devour, find occasion to deceive him. No one is so perfect or so holy but he is sometimes tempted; man cannot be altogether free from temptation.

Yet temptations, though troublesome and severe, are often useful to a man, for in them he is humbled, purified, and instructed. The saints all passed through many temptations and trials to profit by them, while those who could not resist became reprobate and fell away. There is no state so holy, no place so secret that temptations and trials will not come. Man is never safe from them as long as he lives, for they come from within us—in sin we were born. When one temptation or trial passes, another comes; we shall always have something to suffer because we have lost the state of original blessedness.

Many people try to escape temptations, only to fall more deeply. We cannot conquer simply by fleeing, but by patience and true humility we become stronger than all our enemies. The man who only shuns temptations outwardly and does not uproot them will make little progress; indeed they will quickly return, more violent than before.

Little by little, in patience and long-suffering you will overcome them, by the help of God rather than by severity and your own rash ways. Often take counsel when tempted; and do not be harsh with others who are tempted, but console them as you yourself would wish to be consoled.

The beginning of all temptation lies in a wavering mind and little trust in God, for as a rudderless ship is driven hither and yon by waves, so a careless and irresolute man is tempted in many ways.

Fire tempers iron and temptation steels the just.

Often we do not know what we can stand, but temptation shows us what we are.

Above all, we must be especially alert against the beginnings of temptation, for the enemy is more easily conquered if he is refused admittance to the mind and is met beyond the threshold when he knocks.

Someone has said very aptly: "Resist the beginnings; remedies come too late, when by long delay the evil has gained strength." First, a mere

---

[1] Job 7:1.

thought comes to mind, then strong imagination, followed by pleasure, evil delight, and consent. Thus, because he is not resisted in the beginning, Satan gains full entry. And the longer a man delays in resisting, so much the weaker does he become each day, while the strength of the enemy grows against him.

Some suffer great temptations in the beginning of their conversion, others toward the end, while some are troubled almost constantly throughout their life. Others, again, are tempted but lightly according to the wisdom and justice of Divine Providence Who weighs the status and merit of each and prepares all for the salvation of His elect.

We should not despair, therefore, when we are tempted, but pray to God the more fervently that He may see fit to help us, for according to the word of Paul, He will make issue with temptation that we may be able to bear it. Let us humble our souls under the hand of God in every trial and temptation for He will save and exalt the humble in spirit.

In temptations and trials the progress of a man is measured; in them opportunity for merit and virtue is made more manifest.

When a man is not troubled it is not hard for him to be fervent and devout, but if he bears up patiently in time of adversity, there is hope for great progress.

Some, guarded against great temptations, are frequently overcome by small ones in order that, humbled by their weakness in small trials, they may not presume on their own strength in great ones.

The Fourteenth Chapter

AVOIDING RASH JUDGMENT

TURN YOUR attention upon yourself and beware of judging the deeds of other men, for in judging others a man labors vainly, often makes mistakes, and easily sins; whereas, in judging and taking stock of himself he does something that is always profitable.

We frequently judge that things are as we wish them to be, for through personal feeling true perspective is easily lost.

If God were the sole object of our desire, we should not be disturbed so easily by opposition to our opinions. But often something lurks within or happens from without to draw us along with it.

Many, unawares, seek themselves in the things they do. They seem even to enjoy peace of mind when things happen according to their wish and liking, but if otherwise than they desire, they are soon disturbed and saddened. Differences of feeling and opinion often divide friends and acquaintances, even those who are religious and devout.

An old habit is hard to break, and no one is willing to be led farther than he can see.

If you rely more upon your intelligence or industry than upon the virtue of submission to Jesus Christ, you will hardly, and in any case slowly, become an enlightened man. God wants us to be completely subject to Him and, through ardent love, to rise above all human wisdom.

The Fifteenth Chapter

WORKS DONE IN CHARITY

NEVER DO evil for anything in the world, or for the love of any man. For one who is in need, however, a good work may at times be purposely left undone or changed for a better one. This is not the omission of a good deed but rather its improvement.

Without charity external work is of no value, but anything done in charity, be it ever so small and trivial, is entirely fruitful inasmuch as God weighs the love with which a man acts rather than the deed itself.

He does much who loves much. He does much who does a thing well. He does well who serves the common good rather than his own interests.

Now, that which seems to be charity is oftentimes really sensuality, for man's own inclination, his own will, his hope of reward, and his self-interest, are motives seldom absent. On the contrary, he who has true and perfect charity seeks self in nothing, but searches all things for the glory of God. Moreover, he envies no man, because he desires no personal pleasure nor does he wish to rejoice in himself; rather he desires the greater glory of God above all things. He ascribes to man nothing that is good but attributes it wholly to God from Whom all things proceed as from a fountain, and in Whom all the blessed shall rest as their last end and fruition.

If man had but a spark of true charity he would surely sense that all the things of earth are full of vanity!

The Sixteenth Chapter

BEARING WITH THE FAULTS OF OTHERS

UNTIL GOD ordains otherwise, a man ought to bear patiently whatever he cannot correct in himself and in others. Consider it better thus—perhaps to try your patience and to test you, for without such patience and trial your merits are of little account. Nevertheless, under such difficulties you should pray that God will consent to help you bear them calmly.

If, after being admonished once or twice, a person does not amend, do not argue with him but commit the whole matter to God that His will and honor may be furthered in all His servants, for God knows well how to turn evil to good. Try to bear patiently with the defects and infirmities of others, whatever they may be, because you also have many a fault which others must endure.

If you cannot make yourself what you would wish to be, how can you bend others to your will? We want them to be perfect, yet we do not correct our own faults. We wish them to be severely corrected, yet we will not correct ourselves. Their great liberty displeases us, yet we would not be denied what we ask. We would have them bound by laws, yet we will allow ourselves to be restrained in nothing. Hence, it is clear how seldom we think of others as we do of ourselves.

If all were perfect, what should we have to suffer from others for God's sake? But God has so ordained, that we may learn to bear with one another's burdens, for there is no man without fault, no man without burden, no man sufficient to himself nor wise enough. Hence we must support one another, console one another, mutually help, counsel, and advise, for the measure of every man's virtue is best revealed in time of adversity— adversity that does not weaken a man but rather shows what he is.

The Seventeenth Chapter

MONASTIC LIFE

IF YOU wish peace and concord with others, you must learn to break your will in many things. To live in monasteries or religious communities, to remain there without complaint, and to persevere faithfully till death is no small matter. Blessed indeed is he who there lives a good life and there ends his days in happiness.

If you would persevere in seeking perfection, you must consider yourself a pilgrim, an exile on earth. If you would become a religious, you must be content to seem a fool for the sake of Christ. Habit and tonsure change a man but little; it is the change of life, the complete mortification of passions that endow a true religious.

He who seeks anything but God alone and the salvation of his soul will find only trouble and grief, and he who does not try to become the least, the servant of all, cannot remain at peace for long.

You have come to serve, not to rule. You must understand, too, that you have been called to suffer and to work, not to idle and gossip away your time. Here men are tried as gold in a furnace. Here no man can remain unless he desires with all his heart to humble himself before God.

The Eighteenth Chapter

THE EXAMPLE SET US BY
THE HOLY FATHERS

CONSIDER THE lively examples set us by the saints, who possessed the light of true perfection and religion, and you will see how little, how nearly nothing, we do. What, alas, is our life, compared with theirs? The saints and friends of Christ served the Lord in hunger and thirst, in cold and nakedness, in work and fatigue, in vigils and fasts, in prayers and holy meditations, in persecutions and many afflictions. How many and severe were the trials they suffered—the Apostles, martyrs, confessors, virgins, and all the rest who willed to follow in the footsteps of Christ! They hated their lives on earth that they might have life in eternity.

How strict and detached were the lives the holy hermits led in the desert! What long and grave temptations they suffered! How often were they beset by the enemy! What frequent and ardent prayers they offered to God! What rigorous fasts they observed! How great their zeal and their love for spiritual perfection! How brave the fight they waged to master their evil habits! What pure and straightforward purpose they showed toward God! By day they labored and by night they spent themselves in long prayers. Even at work they did not cease from mental prayer. They used all their time profitably; every hour seemed too short for serving God, and in the great sweetness of contemplation, they forgot even their bodily needs.

They renounced all riches, dignities, honors, friends, and associates. They desired nothing of the world. They scarcely allowed themselves the necessities of life, and the service of the body, even when necessary, was irksome to them. They were poor in earthly things but rich in grace and virtue. Outwardly destitute, inwardly they were full of grace and divine consolation. Strangers to the world, they were close and intimate friends of God. To themselves they seemed as nothing, and they were despised by the world, but in the eyes of God they were precious and beloved. They lived in true humility and simple obedience; they walked in charity and patience, making progress daily on the pathway of spiritual life and obtaining great favor with God.

They were given as an example for all religious, and their power to stimulate us to perfection ought to be greater than that of the lukewarm to tempt us to laxity.

How great was the fervor of all religious in the beginning of their holy institution! How great their devotion in prayer and their rivalry for virtue! What splendid discipline flourished among them! What great reverence and obedience in all things under the rule of a superior! The footsteps they left behind still bear witness that they indeed were holy and perfect men who fought bravely and conquered the world.

Today, he who is not a transgressor and who can bear patiently the duties which he has taken upon himself is considered great. How luke-warm and negligent we are! We lose our original fervor very quickly and we even become weary of life from laziness! Do not you, who have seen so many examples of the devout, fall asleep in the pursuit of virtue!

The Nineteenth Chapter

THE PRACTICES OF A GOOD RELIGIOUS

THE LIFE of a good religious ought to abound in every virtue so that he is interiorly what to others he appears to be. With good reason there ought to be much more within than appears on the outside, for He who sees within is God, Whom we ought to reverence most highly wherever we are and in Whose sight we ought to walk pure as the angels.

Each day we ought to renew our resolutions and arouse ourselves to fervor as though it were the first day of our religious life. We ought to say: "Help me, O Lord God, in my good resolution and in Your holy service. Grant me now, this very day, to begin perfectly, for thus far I have done nothing."

As our intention is, so will be our progress; and he who desires perfection must be very diligent. If the strong-willed man fails fre-quently, what of the man who makes up his mind seldom or half-heart-edly? Many are the ways of failing in our resolutions; even a slight omis-sion of religious practice entails a loss of some kind.

Just men depend on the grace of God rather than on their own wis-dom in keeping their resolutions. In Him they confide every undertak-ing, for man, indeed, proposes but God disposes, and God's way is not man's. If an habitual exercise is sometimes omitted out of piety or in the interests of another, it can easily be resumed later. But if it be abandoned carelessly, through weariness or neglect, then the fault is great and will prove hurtful. Much as we try, we still fail too easily in many things. Yet we must always have some fixed purpose, especially against things which beset us the most. Our outward and inward lives alike must be closely watched and well ordered, for both are important to perfection.

If you cannot recollect yourself continuously, do so once a day at least, in the morning or in the evening. In the morning make a resolu-tion and in the evening examine yourself on what you have said this day, what you have done and thought, for in these things perhaps you have often offended God and those about you.

Arm yourself like a man against the devil's assaults. Curb your appetite and you will more easily curb every inclination of the flesh. Never be completely unoccupied, but read or write or pray or meditate or do something for the common good. Bodily discipline, however, must be undertaken with discretion and is not to be practiced indiscriminately by everyone.

Devotions not common to all are not to be displayed in public, for such personal things are better performed in private. Furthermore, beware of indifference to community prayer through love of your own devotions. If, however, after doing completely and faithfully all you are bound and commanded to do, you then have leisure, use it as personal piety suggests.

Not everyone can have the same devotion. One exactly suits this person, another that. Different exercises, likewise, are suitable for different times, some for feast days and some again for weekdays. In time of temptation we need certain devotions. For days of rest and peace we need others. Some are suitable when we are sad, others when we are joyful in the Lord.

About the time of the principal feasts good devotions ought to be renewed and the intercession of the saints more fervently implored. From one feast day to the next we ought to fix our purpose as though we were then to pass from this world and come to the eternal holyday.

During holy seasons, finally, we ought to prepare ourselves carefully, to live holier lives, and to observe each rule more strictly, as though we were soon to receive from God the reward of our labors. If this end be deferred, let us believe that we are not well prepared and that we are not yet worthy of the great glory that shall in due time be revealed to us. Let us try, meanwhile, to prepare ourselves better for death.

"Blessed is the servant," says Christ, "whom his master, when he cometh, shall find watching. Amen I say to you: he shall make him ruler over all his goods."[1]

The Twentieth Chapter

THE LOVE OF SOLITUDE AND SILENCE

SEEK A suitable time for leisure and meditate often on the favors of God. Leave curiosities alone. Read such matters as bring sorrow to the heart rather than occupation to the mind. If you withdraw yourself from unnecessary talking and idle running about, from listening to gossip and rumors, you will find enough time that is suitable for holy meditation.

---

[1] Luke 12:43, 44.

Very many great saints avoided the company of men wherever possible and chose to serve God in retirement. "As often as I have been among men," said one writer, "I have returned less a man." We often find this to be true when we take part in long conversations. It is easier to be silent altogether than not to speak too much. To stay at home is easier than to be sufficiently on guard while away. Anyone, then, who aims to live the inner and spiritual life must go apart, with Jesus, from the crowd.

No man appears in safety before the public eye unless he first relishes obscurity. No man is safe in speaking unless he loves to be silent. No man rules safely unless he is willing to be ruled. No man commands safely unless he has learned well how to obey. No man rejoices safely unless he has within him the testimony of a good conscience.

More than this, the security of the saints was always enveloped in the fear of God, nor were they less cautious and humble because they were conspicuous for great virtues and graces. The security of the wicked, on the contrary, springs from pride and presumption, and will end in their own deception.

Never promise yourself security in this life, even though you seem to be a good religious, or a devout hermit. It happens very often that those whom men esteem highly are more seriously endangered by their own excessive confidence. Hence, for many it is better not to be too free from temptations, but often to be tried lest they become too secure, too filled with pride, or even too eager to fall back upon external comforts.

If only a man would never seek passing joys or entangle himself with worldly affairs, what a good conscience he would have. What great peace and tranquillity would be his, if he cut himself off from all empty care and thought only of things divine, things helpful to his soul, and put all his trust in God.

No man deserves the consolation of heaven unless he persistently arouses himself to holy contrition. If you desire true sorrow of heart, seek the privacy of your cell and shut out the uproar of the world, as it is written: "In your chamber bewail your sins." There you will find what too often you lose abroad.

Your cell will become dear to you if you remain in it, but if you do not, it will become wearisome. If in the beginning of your religious life, you live within your cell and keep to it, it will soon become a special friend and a very great comfort.

In silence and quiet the devout soul advances in virtue and learns the hidden truths of Scripture. There she finds a flood of tears with which to bathe and cleanse herself nightly, that she may become the more intimate with her Creator the farther she withdraws from all the tumult of the world. For God and His holy angels will draw near to him who withdraws from friends and acquaintances.

It is better for a man to be obscure and to attend to his salvation than to neglect it and work miracles. It is praiseworthy for a religious seldom to go abroad, to flee the sight of men and have no wish to see them.

Why wish to see what you are not permitted to have? "The world passes away and the concupiscence thereof." Sensual craving sometimes entices you to wander around, but when the moment is past, what do you bring back with you save a disturbed conscience and heavy heart? A happy going often leads to a sad return, a merry evening to a mournful dawn. Thus, all carnal joy begins sweetly but in the end brings remorse and death.

What can you find elsewhere that you cannot find here in your cell? Behold heaven and earth and all the elements, for of these all things are made. What can you see anywhere under the sun that will remain long? Perhaps you think you will completely satisfy yourself, but you cannot do so, for if you should see all existing things, what would they be but an empty vision?

Raise your eyes to God in heaven and pray because of your sins and shortcomings. Leave vanity to the vain. Set yourself to the things which God has commanded you to do. Close the door upon yourself and call to you Jesus, your Beloved. Remain with Him in your cell, for nowhere else will you find such peace. If you had not left it, and had not listened to idle gossip, you would have remained in greater peace. But since you love, sometimes, to hear news, it is only right that you should suffer sorrow of heart from it.

The Twenty-First Chapter

SORROW OF HEART

IF YOU wish to make progress in virtue, live in the fear of the Lord, do not look for too much freedom, discipline your senses, and shun inane silliness. Sorrow opens the door to many a blessing which dissoluteness usually destroys.

It is a wonder that any man who considers and meditates on his exiled state and the many dangers to his soul, can ever be perfectly happy in this life. Lighthearted and heedless of our defects, we do not feel the real sorrows of our souls, but often indulge in empty laughter when we have good reason to weep. No liberty is true and no joy is genuine unless it is founded in the fear of the Lord and a good conscience.

Happy is the man who can throw off the weight of every care and recollect himself in holy contrition. Happy is the man who casts from him all that can stain or burden his conscience.

Fight like a man. Habit is overcome by habit.

If you leave men alone, they will leave you alone to do what you have to do. Do not busy yourself about the affairs of others and do not become entangled in the business of your superiors. Keep an eye primarily on yourself and admonish yourself instead of your friends.

If you do not enjoy the favor of men, do not let it sadden you; but consider it a serious matter if you do not conduct yourself as well or as carefully as is becoming for a servant of God and a devout religious.

It is often better and safer for us to have few consolations in this life, especially comforts of the body. Yet if we do not have divine consolation or experience it rarely, it is our own fault because we seek no sorrow of heart and do not forsake vain outward satisfaction.

Consider yourself unworthy of divine solace and deserving rather of much tribulation. When a man is perfectly contrite, the whole world is bitter and wearisome to him.

A good man always finds enough over which to mourn and weep; whether he thinks of himself or of his neighbor he knows that no one lives here without suffering, and the closer he examines himself the more he grieves.

The sins and vices in which we are so entangled that we can rarely apply ourselves to the contemplation of heaven are matters for just sorrow and inner remorse.

I do not doubt that you would correct yourself more earnestly if you would think more of an early death than of a long life. And if you pondered in your heart the future pains of hell or of purgatory, I believe you would willingly endure labor and trouble and would fear no hardship. But since these thoughts never pierce the heart and since we are enamored of flattering pleasure, we remain very cold and indifferent. Our wretched body complains so easily because our soul is altogether too lifeless.

Pray humbly to the Lord, therefore, that He may give you the spirit of contrition and say with the Prophet: "Feed me, Lord, with the bread of mourning and give me to drink of tears in full measure."[1]

The Twenty-Second Chapter

THOUGHTS ON THE MISERY OF MAN

WHEREVER YOU are, wherever you go, you are miserable unless you turn to God. So why be dismayed when things do not happen as you wish and desire? Is there anyone who has everything as he wishes?

---

[1] Ps. 79:6.

No—neither I, nor you, nor any man on earth. There is no one in the world, be he Pope or king, who does not suffer trial and anguish.

Who is the better off then? Surely, it is the man who will suffer something for God. Many unstable and weak-minded people say: "See how well that man lives, how rich, how great he is, how powerful and mighty." But you must lift up your eyes to the riches of heaven and realize that the material goods of which they speak are nothing. These things are uncertain and very burdensome because they are never possessed without anxiety and fear. Man's happiness does not consist in the possession of abundant goods; a very little is enough.

Living on earth is truly a misery. The more a man desires spiritual life, the more bitter the present becomes to him, because he understands better and sees more clearly the defects, the corruption of human nature. To eat and drink, to watch and sleep, to rest, to labor, and to be bound by other human necessities is certainly a great misery and affliction to the devout man who would gladly be released from them and be free from all sin. Truly, the inner man is greatly burdened in this world by the necessities of the body, and for this reason the Prophet prayed that he might be as free from them as possible, when he said: "From my necessities, O Lord, deliver me."[1]

But woe to those who know not their own misery, and greater woe to those who love this miserable and corruptible life. Some, indeed, can scarcely procure its necessities either by work or by begging; yet they love it so much that, if they could live here always, they would care nothing for the kingdom of God.

How foolish and faithless of heart are those who are so engrossed in earthly things as to relish nothing but what is carnal! Miserable men indeed, for in the end they will see to their sorrow how cheap and worthless was the thing they loved.

The saints of God and all devout friends of Christ did not look to what pleases the body nor to the things that are popular from time to time. Their whole hope and aim centered on the everlasting good. Their whole desire pointed upward to the lasting and invisible realm, lest the love of what is visible drag them down to lower things.

Do not lose heart, then, my brother, in pursuing your spiritual life. There is yet time, and your hour is not past. Why delay your purpose? Arise! Begin at once and say: "Now is the time to act, now is the time to fight, now is the proper time to amend."

When you are troubled and afflicted, that is the time to gain merit.

---

[1] Ps. 24:17.

You must pass through water and fire before coming to rest. Unless you do violence to yourself you will not overcome vice.

So long as we live in this fragile body, we can neither be free from sin nor live without weariness and sorrow. Gladly would we rest from all misery, but in losing innocence through sin we also lost true blessedness. Therefore, we must have patience and await the mercy of God until this iniquity passes, until mortality is swallowed up in life.

How great is the frailty of human nature which is ever prone to evil! Today you confess your sins and tomorrow you again commit the sins which you confessed. One moment you resolve to be careful, and yet after an hour you act as though you had made no resolution.

We have cause, therefore, because of our frailty and feebleness, to humble ourselves and never think anything great of ourselves. Through neglect we may quickly lose that which by God's grace we have acquired only through long, hard labor. What, eventually, will become of us who so quickly grow lukewarm? Woe to us if we presume to rest in peace and security when actually there is no true holiness in our lives. It would be beneficial for us, like good novices, to be instructed once more in the principles of a good life, to see if there be hope of amendment and greater spiritual progress in the future.

The Twenty-Third Chapter

THOUGHTS ON DEATH

VERY SOON your life here will end; consider, then, what may be in store for you elsewhere. Today we live; tomorrow we die and are quickly forgotten. Oh, the dullness and hardness of a heart which looks only to the present instead of preparing for that which is to come!

Therefore, in every deed and every thought, act as though you were to die this very day. If you had a good conscience you would not fear death very much. It is better to avoid sin than to fear death. If you are not prepared today, how will you be prepared tomorrow? Tomorrow is an uncertain day; how do you know you will have a tomorrow?

What good is it to live a long life when we amend that life so little? Indeed, a long life does not always benefit us, but on the contrary, frequently adds to our guilt. Would that in this world we had lived well throughout one single day. Many count up the years they have spent in religion but find their lives made little holier. If it is so terrifying to die, it is nevertheless possible that to live longer is more dangerous. Blessed is he who keeps the moment of death ever before his eyes and prepares for it every day.

If you have ever seen a man die, remember that you, too, must go the same way. In the morning consider that you may not live till evening, and when evening comes do not dare to promise yourself the dawn. Be always ready, therefore, and so live that death will never take you unprepared. Many die suddenly and unexpectedly, for in the unexpected hour the Son of God will come. When that last moment arrives you will begin to have a quite different opinion of the life that is now entirely past and you will regret very much that you were so careless and remiss.

How happy and prudent is he who tries now in life to be what he wants to be found in death. Perfect contempt of the world, a lively desire to advance in virtue, a love for discipline, the works of penance, readiness to obey, self-denial, and the endurance of every hardship for the love of Christ, these will give a man great expectations of a happy death.

You can do many good works when in good health; what can you do when you are ill? Few are made better by sickness. Likewise they who undertake many pilgrimages seldom become holy.

Do not put your trust in friends and relatives, and do not put off the care of your soul till later, for men will forget you more quickly than you think. It is better to provide now, in time, and send some good account ahead of you than to rely on the help of others. If you do not care for your own welfare now, who will care when you are gone?

The present is very precious; these are the days of salvation; now is the acceptable time. How sad that you do not spend the time in which you might purchase everlasting life in a better way. The time will come when you will want just one day, just one hour in which to make amends, and do you know whether you will obtain it?

See, then, dearly beloved, the great danger from which you can free yourself and the great fear from which you can be saved, if only you will always be wary and mindful of death. Try to live now in such a manner that at the moment of death you may be glad rather than fearful. Learn to die to the world now, that then you may begin to live with Christ. Learn to spurn all things now, that then you may freely go to Him. Chastise your body in penance now, that then you may have the confidence born of certainty.

Ah, foolish man, why do you plan to live long when you are not sure of living even a day? How many have been deceived and suddenly snatched away! How often have you heard of persons being killed by drownings, by fatal falls from high places, of persons dying at meals, at play, in fires, by the sword, in pestilence, or at the hands of robbers! Death is the end of everyone and the life of man quickly passes away like a shadow.

Who will remember you when you are dead? Who will pray for you? Do now, beloved, what you can, because you do not know when you will die, nor what your fate will be after death. Gather for yourself the riches of immortality while you have time. Think of nothing but your salvation.

Care only for the things of God. Make friends for yourself now by honoring the saints of God, by imitating their actions, so that when you depart this life they may receive you into everlasting dwellings.

Keep yourself as a stranger here on earth, a pilgrim whom its affairs do not concern at all. Keep your heart free and raise it up to God, for you have not here a lasting home. To Him direct your daily prayers, your sighs and tears, that your soul may merit after death to pass in happiness to the Lord.

The Twenty-Fourth Chapter

JUDGMENT AND THE PUNISHMENT OF SIN

IN ALL things consider the end; how you shall stand before the strict Judge from Whom nothing is hidden and Who will pronounce judgment in all justice, accepting neither bribes nor excuses. And you, miserable and wretched sinner, who fear even the countenance of an angry man, what answer will you make to the God Who knows all your sins? Why do you not provide for yourself against the day of judgment when no man can be excused or defended by another because each will have enough to do to answer for himself? In this life your work is profitable, your tears acceptable, your sighs audible, your sorrow satisfying and purifying.

The patient man goes through a great and salutary purgatory when he grieves more over the malice of one who harms him than for his own injury; when he prays readily for his enemies and forgives offenses from his heart; when he does not hesitate to ask pardon of others; when he is more easily moved to pity than to anger; when he does frequent violence to himself and tries to bring the body into complete subjection to the spirit.

It is better to atone for sin now and to cut away vices than to keep them for purgation in the hereafter. In truth, we deceive ourselves by our ill-advised love of the flesh. What will that fire feed upon but our sins? The more we spare ourselves now and the more we satisfy the flesh, the harder will the reckoning be and the more we keep for the burning.

For a man will be more grievously punished in the things in which he has sinned. There the lazy will be driven with burning prongs, and gluttons tormented with unspeakable hunger and thirst; the wanton and lust-loving will be bathed in burning pitch and foul brimstone; the envious will howl in their grief like mad dogs.

Every vice will have its own proper punishment. The proud will be faced with every confusion and the avaricious pinched with the most abject want. One hour of suffering there will be more bitter than a hundred years of the most severe penance here. In this life men sometimes rest from work and enjoy the comfort of friends, but the damned have no rest or consolation.

You must, therefore, take care and repent of your sins now so that on the day of judgment you may rest secure with the blessed. For on that day the just will stand firm against those who tortured and oppressed them, and he who now submits humbly to the judgment of men will arise to pass judgment upon them. The poor and humble will have great confidence, while the proud will be struck with fear. He who learned to be a fool in this world and to be scorned for Christ will then appear to have been wise.

In that day every trial borne in patience will be pleasing and the voice of iniquity will be stilled; the devout will be glad; the irreligious will mourn; and the mortified body will rejoice far more than if it had been pampered with every pleasure. Then the cheap garment will shine with splendor and the rich one become faded and worn; the poor cottage will be more praised than the gilded palace. In that day persevering patience will count more than all the power in this world; simple obedience will be exalted above all worldly cleverness; a good and clean conscience will gladden the heart of man far more than the philosophy of the learned; and contempt for riches will be of more weight than every treasure on earth.

Then you will find more consolation in having prayed devoutly than in having fared daintily; you will be happy that you preferred silence to prolonged gossip.

Then holy works will be of greater value than many fair words; strictness of life and hard penances will be more pleasing than all earthly delights.

Learn, then, to suffer little things now that you may not have to suffer greater ones in eternity. Prove here what you can bear hereafter. If you can suffer only a little now, how will you be able to endure eternal torment? If a little suffering makes you impatient now, what will hell fire do? In truth, you cannot have two joys: you cannot taste the pleasures of this world and afterward reign with Christ.

If your life to this moment had been full of honors and pleasures, what good would it do if at this instant you should die? All is vanity, therefore, except to love God and to serve Him alone.

He who loves God with all his heart does not fear death or punishment or judgment or hell, because perfect love assures access to God.

It is no wonder that he who still delights in sin fears death and judgment.

It is good, however, that even if love does not as yet restrain you from evil, at least the fear of hell does. The man who casts aside the fear of God cannot continue long in goodness but will quickly fall into the snares of the devil.

The Twenty-Fifth Chapter

ZEAL IN AMENDING OUR LIVES

BE WATCHFUL and diligent in God's service and often think of why you left the world and came here. Was it not that you might live for God and become a spiritual man? Strive earnestly for perfection, then, because in a short time you will receive the reward of your labor, and neither fear nor sorrow shall come upon you at the hour of death.

Labor a little now, and soon you shall find great rest, in truth, eternal joy; for if you continue faithful and diligent in doing, God will undoubtedly be faithful and generous in rewarding. Continue to have reasonable hope of gaining salvation, but do not act as though you were certain of it lest you grow indolent and proud.

One day when a certain man who wavered often and anxiously between hope and fear was struck with sadness, he knelt in humble prayer before the altar of a church. While meditating on these things, he said: "Oh if I but knew whether I should persevere to the end!" Instantly he heard within the divine answer: "If you knew this, what would you do? Do now what you would do then and you will be quite secure." Immediately consoled and comforted, he resigned himself to the divine will and the anxious uncertainty ceased. His curiosity no longer sought to know what the future held for him, and he tried instead to find the perfect, the acceptable will of God in the beginning and end of every good work.

"Trust thou in the Lord and do good," says the Prophet; "dwell in the land and thou shalt feed on its riches."[1]

There is one thing that keeps many from zealously improving their lives, that is, dread of the difficulty, the toil of battle. Certainly they who try manfully to overcome the most difficult and unpleasant obstacles far outstrip others in the pursuit of virtue. A man makes the most progress and merits the most grace precisely in those matters wherein he gains the greatest victories over self and most mortifies his will. True, each one has his own difficulties to meet and conquer, but a diligent and sincere man will make greater progress even though he have more

[1] Ps. 36:3.

passions than one who is more even-tempered but less concerned about virtue.

Two things particularly further improvement—to withdraw oneself forcibly from those vices to which nature is viciously inclined, and to work fervently for those graces which are most needed.

Study also to guard against and to overcome the faults which in others very frequently displease you. Make the best of every opportunity, so that if you see or hear good example you may be moved to imitate it. On the other hand, take care lest you be guilty of those things which you consider reprehensible, or if you have ever been guilty of them, try to correct yourself as soon as possible. As you see others, so they see you.

How pleasant and sweet to behold brethren fervent and devout, well mannered and disciplined! How sad and painful to see them wandering in dissolution, not practicing the things to which they are called! How hurtful it is to neglect the purpose of their vocation and to attend to what is not their business!

Remember the purpose you have undertaken, and keep in mind the image of the Crucified. Even though you may have walked for many years on the pathway to God, you may well be ashamed if, with the image of Christ before you, you do not try to make yourself still more like Him.

The religious who concerns himself intently and devoutly with our Lord's most holy life and passion will find there an abundance of all things useful and necessary for him. He need not seek for anything better than Jesus.

If the Crucified should come to our hearts, how quickly and abundantly we would learn!

A fervent religious accepts all the things that are commanded him and does them well, but a negligent and lukewarm religious has trial upon trial, and suffers anguish from every side because he has no consolation within and is forbidden to seek it from without. The religious who does not live up to his rule exposes himself to dreadful ruin, and he who wishes to be more free and untrammeled will always be in trouble, for something or other will always displease him.

How do so many other religious who are confined in cloistered discipline get along? They seldom go out, they live in contemplation, their food is poor, their clothing coarse, they work hard, they speak but little, keep long vigils, rise early, pray much, read frequently, and subject themselves to all sorts of discipline. Think of the Carthusians and the Cistercians, the monks and nuns of different orders, how every night they rise to sing praise to the Lord. It were a shame that you should grow lazy in such holy service when so many religious have already begun to rejoice in God.

If there were nothing else to do but praise the Lord God with all your heart and voice, if you had never to eat, or drink, or sleep, but could praise God always and occupy yourself solely with spiritual pursuits, how much happier you would be than you are now, a slave to every necessity of the body! Would that there were no such needs, but only the spiritual refreshments of the soul which, sad to say, we taste too seldom!

When a man reaches a point where he seeks no solace from any creature, then he begins to relish God perfectly. Then also he will be content no matter what may happen to him. He will neither rejoice over great things nor grieve over small ones, but will place himself entirely and confidently in the hands of God, Who for him is all in all, to Whom nothing ever perishes or dies, for Whom all things live, and Whom they serve as He desires.

Always remember your end and do not forget that lost time never returns. Without care and diligence you will never acquire virtue. When you begin to grow lukewarm, you are falling into the beginning of evil; but if you give yourself to fervor, you will find peace and will experience less hardship because of God's grace and the love of virtue.

A fervent and diligent man is ready for all things. It is greater work to resist vices and passions than to sweat in physical toil. He who does not overcome small faults, shall fall little by little into greater ones.

If you have spent the day profitably, you will always be happy at eventide. Watch over yourself, arouse yourself, warn yourself, and regardless of what becomes of others, do not neglect yourself. The more violence you do to yourself, the more progress you will make.

BOOK TWO

THE INTERIOR LIFE

The First Chapter

MEDITATION

THE KINGDOM of God is within you," says the Lord.[1]

Turn, then, to God with all your heart. Forsake this wretched world and your soul shall find rest. Learn to despise external things, to devote yourself to those that are within, and you will see the kingdom of God come unto you, that kingdom which is peace and joy in the Holy Spirit, gifts not given to the impious.

Christ will come to you offering His consolation, if you prepare a fit dwelling for Him in your heart, whose beauty and glory, wherein He takes delight, are all from within. His visits with the inward man are frequent, His communion sweet and full of consolation, His peace great, and His intimacy wonderful indeed.

Therefore, faithful soul, prepare your heart for this Bridegroom that He may come and dwell within you; He Himself says: "If any one love Me, he will keep My word, and My Father will love him, and We will come to him, and will make Our abode with him."[2]

Give place, then, to Christ, but deny entrance to all others, for when you have Christ you are rich and He is sufficient for you. He will

---

[1] Luke 17:21.
[2] John 14:23.

28

provide for you. He will supply your every want, so that you need not trust in frail, changeable men. Christ remains forever, standing firmly with us to the end.

Do not place much confidence in weak and mortal man, helpful and friendly though he be; and do not grieve too much if he sometimes opposes and contradicts you. Those who are with us today may be against us tomorrow, and vice versa, for men change with the wind. Place all your trust in God; let Him be your fear and your love. He will answer for you; He will do what is best for you.

You have here no lasting home. You are a stranger and a pilgrim wherever you may be, and you shall have no rest until you are wholly united with Christ.

Why do you look about here when this is not the place of your repose? Dwell rather upon heaven and give but a passing glance to all earthly things. They all pass away, you together with them. Take care, then, that you do not cling to them lest you be entrapped and perish. Fix your mind on the Most High, and pray unceasingly to Christ.

If you do not know how to meditate on heavenly things, direct your thoughts to Christ's passion and willingly behold His sacred wounds. If you turn devoutly to the wounds and precious stigmata of Christ, you will find great comfort in suffering, you will mind but little the scorn of men, and you will easily bear their slanderous talk.

When Christ was in the world, He was despised by men; in the hour of need He was forsaken by acquaintances and left by friends to the depths of scorn. He was willing to suffer and to be despised; do you dare to complain of anything? He had enemies and defamers; do you want everyone to be your friend, your benefactor? How can your patience be rewarded if no adversity test it? How can you be a friend of Christ if you are not willing to suffer any hardship? Suffer with Christ and for Christ if you wish to reign with Him.

Had you but once entered into perfect communion with Jesus or tasted a little of His ardent love, you would care nothing at all for your own comfort or discomfort but would rejoice in the reproach you suffer; for love of Him makes a man despise himself.

A man who is a lover of Jesus and of truth, a truly interior man who is free from uncontrolled affections, can turn to God at will and rise above himself to enjoy spiritual peace.

He who tastes life as it really is, not as men say or think it is, is indeed wise with the wisdom of God rather than of men.

He who learns to live the interior life and to take little account of outward things, does not seek special places or times to perform devout exercises. A spiritual man quickly recollects himself because he has never wasted his attention upon externals. No outside work, no business that cannot wait stands in his way. He adjusts himself to things as they happen. He whose disposition is well ordered cares nothing about the strange, perverse behavior of others, for a man is upset and distracted only in proportion as he engrosses himself in externals.

If all were well with you, therefore, and if you were purified from all sin, everything would tend to your good and be to your profit. But because you are as yet neither entirely dead to self nor free from all earthly affection, there is much that often displeases and disturbs you. Nothing so mars and defiles the heart of man as impure attachment to created things. But if you refuse external consolation, you will be able to contemplate heavenly things and often to experience interior joy.

The Second Chapter

HUMILITY

BE NOT troubled about those who are with you or against you, but take care that God be with you in everything you do. Keep your conscience clear and God will protect you, for the malice of man cannot harm one whom God wishes to help. If you know how to suffer in silence, you will undoubtedly experience God's help. He knows when and how to deliver you; therefore, place yourself in His hands, for it is a divine prerogative to help men and free them from all distress.

It is often good for us to have others know our faults and rebuke them, for it gives us greater humility. When a man humbles himself because of his faults, he easily placates those about him and readily appeases those who are angry with him.

It is the humble man whom God protects and liberates; it is the humble whom He loves and consoles. To the humble He turns and upon them bestows great grace, that after their humiliation He may raise them up to glory. He reveals His secrets to the humble, and with kind invitation bids them come to Him. Thus, the humble man enjoys peace in the midst of many vexations, because his trust is in God, not in the world. Hence, you must not think that you have made any progress until you look upon yourself as inferior to all others.

The Third Chapter

GOODNESS AND PEACE IN MAN

FIRST KEEP peace with yourself; then you will be able to bring peace to others.

A peaceful man does more good than a learned man. Whereas a passionate man turns even good to evil and is quick to believe evil, the peaceful man, being good himself, turns all things to good.

The man who is at perfect ease is never suspicious, but the disturbed and discontented spirit is upset by many a suspicion. He neither rests himself nor permits others to do so. He often says what ought not to be said and leaves undone what ought to be done. He is concerned with the duties of others but neglects his own.

Direct your zeal, therefore, first upon yourself; then you may with justice exercise it upon those about you. You are well versed in coloring your own actions with excuses which you will not accept from others, though it would be more just to accuse yourself and excuse your brother. If you wish men to bear with you, you must bear with them. Behold, how far you are from true charity and humility which does not know how to be angry with anyone, or to be indignant save only against self!

It is no great thing to associate with the good and gentle, for such association is naturally pleasing. Everyone enjoys a peaceful life and prefers persons of congenial habits. But to be able to live at peace with harsh and perverse men, or with the undisciplined and those who irritate us, is a great grace, a praiseworthy and manly thing.

Some people live at peace with themselves and with their fellow men, but others are never at peace with themselves nor do they bring it to anyone else. These latter are a burden to everyone, but they are more of a burden to themselves. A few, finally, live at peace with themselves and try to restore it to others.

Now, all our peace in this miserable life is found in humbly enduring suffering rather than in being free from it. He who knows best how to suffer will enjoy the greater peace, because he is the conqueror of himself, the master of the world, a friend of Christ, and an heir of heaven.

The Fourth Chapter

PURITY OF MIND AND UNITY OF PURPOSE

A MAN is raised up from the earth by two wings—simplicity and purity. There must be simplicity in his intention and purity in his desires. Simplicity leads to God, purity embraces and enjoys Him.

If your heart be free from ill-ordered affection, no good deed will be difficult for you. If you aim at and seek after nothing but the pleasure of God and the welfare of your neighbor, you will enjoy freedom within.

If your heart were right, then every created thing would be a mirror of life for you and a book of holy teaching, for there is no creature so small and worthless that it does not show forth the goodness of God. If inwardly you were good and pure, you would see all things clearly and understand them rightly, for a pure heart penetrates to heaven and hell, and as a man is within, so he judges what is without. If there be joy in the world, the pure of heart certainly possess it; and if there be anguish and affliction anywhere, an evil conscience knows it too well.

As iron cast into fire loses its rust and becomes glowing white, so he who turns completely to God is stripped of his sluggishness and changed into a new man. When a man begins to grow lax, he fears a little toil and welcomes external comfort, but when he begins perfectly to conquer himself and to walk manfully in the ways of God, then he thinks those things less difficult which he thought so hard before.

The Fifth Chapter

OURSELVES

WE MUST not rely too much upon ourselves, for grace and understanding are often lacking in us. We have but little inborn light, and this we quickly lose through negligence. Often we are not aware that we are so blind in heart. Meanwhile we do wrong, and then do worse in excusing it. At times we are moved by passion, and we think it zeal. We take others to task for small mistakes, and overlook greater ones in ourselves. We are quick enough to feel and brood over the things we suffer from others, but we think nothing of how much others suffer from us. If a man would weigh his own deeds fully and rightly, he would find little cause to pass severe judgment on others.

The interior man puts the care of himself before all other concerns, and he who attends to himself carefully does not find it hard to hold his tongue about others. You will never be devout of heart unless you are thus silent about the affairs of others and pay particular attention to yourself. If you attend wholly to God and yourself, you will be little disturbed by what you see about you.

Where are your thoughts when they are not upon yourself? And after attending to various things, what have you gained if you have neglected self? If you wish to have true peace of mind and unity of purpose, you must cast all else aside and keep only yourself before your eyes.

You will make great progress if you keep yourself free from all temporal cares, for to value anything that is temporal is a great mistake. Consider nothing great, nothing high, nothing pleasing, nothing acceptable, except God Himself or that which is of God. Consider the consolations of creatures as vanity, for the soul that loves God scorns all things that are inferior to Him. God alone, the eternal and infinite, satisfies all, bringing comfort to the soul and true joy to the body.

The Sixth Chapter

THE JOY OF A GOOD CONSCIENCE

THE GLORY of a good man is the testimony of a good conscience. Therefore, keep your conscience good and you will always enjoy happiness, for a good conscience can bear a great deal and can bring joy even in the midst of adversity. But an evil conscience is ever restive and fearful.

Sweet shall be your rest if your heart does not reproach you.

Do not rejoice unless you have done well. Sinners never experience true interior joy or peace, for "there is no peace to the wicked," says the Lord.[1] Even if they say: "We are at peace, no evil shall befall us and no one dares to hurt us," do not believe them; for the wrath of God will arise quickly, and their deeds will be brought to naught and their thoughts will perish.

To glory in adversity is not hard for the man who loves, for this is to glory in the cross of the Lord. But the glory given or received of men is short lived, and the glory of the world is ever companioned by sorrow. The glory of the good, however, is in their conscience and not in the lips of men, for the joy of the just is from God and in God, and their gladness is founded on truth.

The man who longs for the true, eternal glory does not care for that of time; and he who seeks passing fame or does not in his heart despise it, undoubtedly cares little for the glory of heaven.

---

[1] Isa. 48:22.

He who minds neither praise nor blame possesses great peace of heart and, if his conscience is good, he will easily be contented and at peace.

Praise adds nothing to your holiness, nor does blame take anything from it. You are what you are, and you cannot be said to be better than you are in God's sight. If you consider well what you are within, you will not care what men say about you. They look to appearances but God looks to the heart. They consider the deed but God weighs the motive.

It is characteristic of a humble soul always to do good and to think little of itself. It is a mark of great purity and deep faith to look for no consolation in created things. The man who desires no justification from without has clearly entrusted himself to God: "For not he who commendeth himself is approved," says St. Paul, "but he whom God commendeth."[2]

To walk with God interiorly, to be free from any external affection—this is the state of the inward man.

The Seventh Chapter

LOVING JESUS ABOVE ALL THINGS

BLESSED IS he who appreciates what it is to love Jesus and who despises himself for the sake of Jesus. Give up all other love for His, since He wishes to be loved alone above all things.

Affection for creatures is deceitful and inconstant, but the love of Jesus is true and enduring. He who clings to a creature will fall with its frailty, but he who gives himself to Jesus will ever be strengthened.

Love Him, then; keep Him as a friend. He will not leave you as others do, or let you suffer lasting death. Sometime, whether you will or not, you will have to part with everything. Cling, therefore, to Jesus in life and death; trust yourself to the glory of Him who alone can help you when all others fail.

Your Beloved is such that He will not accept what belongs to another—He wants your heart for Himself alone, to be enthroned therein as King in His own right. If you but knew how to free yourself entirely from all creatures, Jesus would gladly dwell within you.

You will find, apart from Him, that nearly all the trust you place in men is a total loss. Therefore, neither confide in nor depend upon a wind-shaken reed, for "all flesh is grass"[1] and all its glory, like the flower of grass, will fade away.

---

[2] II Cor. 10:18.

---

[1] Isa. 15:6.

You will quickly be deceived if you look only to the outward appearance of men, and you will often be disappointed if you seek comfort and gain in them. If, however, you seek Jesus in all things, you will surely find Him. Likewise, if you seek yourself, you will find yourself—to your own ruin. For the man who does not seek Jesus does himself much greater harm than the whole world and all his enemies could ever do.

The Eighth Chapter

THE INTIMATE FRIENDSHIP OF JESUS

WHEN JESUS is near, all is well and nothing seems difficult. When He is absent, all is hard. When Jesus does not speak within, all other comfort is empty, but if He says only a word, it brings great consolation.

Did not Mary Magdalen rise at once from her weeping when Martha said to her: "The Master is come, and calleth for thee"?[1] Happy is the hour when Jesus calls one from tears to joy of spirit.

How dry and hard you are without Jesus! How foolish and vain if you desire anything but Him! Is it not a greater loss than losing the whole world? For what, without Jesus, can the world give you? Life without Him is a relentless hell, but living with Him is a sweet paradise. If Jesus be with you, no enemy can harm you.

He who finds Jesus finds a rare treasure, indeed, a good above every good, whereas he who loses Him loses more than the whole world. The man who lives without Jesus is the poorest of the poor, whereas no one is so rich as the man who lives in His grace.

It is a great art to know how to converse with Jesus, and great wisdom to know how to keep Him. Be humble and peaceful, and Jesus will be with you. Be devout and calm, and He will remain with you. You may quickly drive Him away and lose His grace, if you turn back to the outside world. And, if you drive Him away and lose Him, to whom will you go and whom will you then seek as a friend? You cannot live well without a friend, and if Jesus be not your friend above all else, you will be very sad and desolate. Thus, you are acting foolishly if you trust or rejoice in any other. Choose the opposition of the whole world rather than offend Jesus. Of all those who are dear to you, let Him be your special love. Let all things be loved for the sake of Jesus, but Jesus for His own sake.

Jesus Christ must be loved alone with a special love for He alone, of

---

[1] John 11:28.

all friends, is good and faithful. For Him and in Him you must love friends and foes alike, and pray to Him that all may know and love Him.

Never desire special praise or love, for that belongs to God alone Who has no equal. Never wish that anyone's affection be centered in you, nor let yourself be taken up with the love of anyone, but let Jesus be in you and in every good man. Be pure and free within, unentangled with any creature.

You must bring to God a clean and open heart if you wish to attend and see how sweet the Lord is. Truly you will never attain this happiness unless His grace prepares you and draws you on so that you may forsake all things to be united with Him alone.

When the grace of God comes to a man he can do all things, but when it leaves him he becomes poor and weak, abandoned, as it were, to affliction. Yet, in this condition he should not become dejected or despair. On the contrary, he should calmly await the will of God and bear whatever befalls him in praise of Jesus Christ, for after winter comes summer, after night, the day, and after the storm, a great calm.

The Ninth Chapter

WANTING NO SHARE IN COMFORT

IT IS not hard to spurn human consolation when we have the divine. It is, however, a very great thing indeed to be able to live without either divine or human comforting and for the honor of God willingly to endure this exile of heart, not to seek oneself in anything, and to think nothing of one's own merit.

Does it matter much, if at the coming of grace, you are cheerful and devout? This is an hour desired by all, for he whom the grace of God sustains travels easily enough. What wonder if he feel no burden when borne up by the Almighty and led on by the Supreme Guide! For we are always glad to have something to comfort us, and only with difficulty does a man divest himself of self.

The holy martyr, Lawrence, with his priest, conquered the world because he despised everything in it that seemed pleasing to him, and for love of Christ patiently suffered the great high priest of God, Sixtus, whom he loved dearly, to be taken from him. Thus, by his love for the Creator he overcame the love of man, and chose instead of human consolation the good pleasure of God. So you, too, must learn to part with an intimate and much-needed friend for the love of God. Do not take it to heart when you are deserted by a friend, knowing that in the end we must all be parted from one another.

A man must fight long and bravely against himself before he learns to master himself fully and to direct all his affections toward God. When he trusts in himself, he easily takes to human consolation. The true lover of Christ, however, who sincerely pursues virtue, does not fall back upon consolations nor seek such pleasures of sense, but prefers severe trials and hard labors for the sake of Christ.

When, therefore, spiritual consolation is given by God, receive it gratefully, but understand that it is His gift and not your meriting. Do not exult, do not be overjoyed, do not be presumptuous, but be the humbler for the gift, more careful and wary in all your actions, for this hour will pass and temptation will come in its wake.

When consolation is taken away, do not at once despair but wait humbly and patiently for the heavenly visit, since God can restore to you more abundant solace.

This is neither new nor strange to one who knows God's ways, for such change of fortune often visited the great saints and prophets of old. Thus there was one who, when grace was with him, declared: "In my prosperity I said: 'I shall never be moved.'" But when grace was taken away, he adds what he experienced in himself: "Thou didst hide Thy face, and I was troubled." Meanwhile he does not despair; rather he prays more earnestly to the Lord, saying: "To Thee, O Lord, will I cry; and I will make supplication to my God." At length, he receives the fruit of his prayer, and testifying that he was heard, says "The Lord hath heard, and hath had mercy on me: the Lord became my helper." And how was he helped? "Thou hast turned," he says, "my mourning into joy, and hast surrounded me with gladness."[1]

If this is the case with great saints, we who are weak and poor ought not to despair because we are fervent at times and at other times cold, for the spirit comes and goes according to His will. Of this the blessed Job declared: "Thou visitest him early in the morning, and Thou provest him suddenly."[2]

In what can I hope, then, or in whom ought I trust, save only in the great mercy of God and the hope of heavenly grace? For though I have with me good men, devout brethren, faithful friends, holy books, beautiful treatises, sweet songs and hymns, all these help and please but little when I am abandoned by grace and left to my poverty. At such times there is no better remedy than patience and resignation of self to the will of God.

---

[1] Ps. 29:7–12.
[2] Job 7:18.

I have never met a man so religious and devout that he has not experienced at some time a withdrawal of grace and felt a lessening of fervor. No saint was so sublimely rapt and enlightened as not to be tempted before and after. He, indeed, is not worthy of the sublime contemplation of God who has not been tried by some tribulation for the sake of God. For temptation is usually the sign preceding the consolation that is to follow, and heavenly consolation is promised to all those proved by temptation. "To him that overcometh," says Christ, "I will give to eat of the Tree of Life."[3] Divine consolation, then, is given in order to make a man braver in enduring adversity, and temptation follows in order that he may not pride himself on the good he has done.

The devil does not sleep, nor is the flesh yet dead; therefore, you must never cease your preparation for battle, because on the right and on the left are enemies who never rest.

The Tenth Chapter

APPRECIATING GOD'S GRACE

WHY DO you look for rest when you were born to work? Resign yourself to patience rather than to comfort, to carrying your cross rather than to enjoyment.

What man in the world, if he could always have them, would not readily accept consolation and spiritual joy, benefits which excel all earthly delights and pleasures of the body? The latter, indeed, are either vain or base, while spiritual joys, born of virtue and infused by God into pure minds, are alone truly pleasant and noble.

Now, since the moment of temptation is always nigh, since false freedom of mind and overconfidence in self are serious obstacles to these visitations from heaven, a man can never enjoy them just as he wishes.

God does well in giving the grace of consolation, but man does evil in not returning everything gratefully to God. Thus, the gifts of grace cannot flow in us when we are ungrateful to the Giver, when we do not return them to the Fountainhead. Grace is always given to him who is duly grateful, and what is wont to be given the humble will be taken away from the proud.

I do not desire consolation that robs me of contrition, nor do I care for contemplation that leads to pride, for not all that is high is holy, nor is all that is sweet good, nor every desire pure, nor all that is dear to us

---

[3] Apoc. 2:7.

pleasing to God. I accept willingly the grace whereby I become more humble and contrite, more willing to renounce self.

The man who has been taught by the gift of grace, and who learns by the lash of its withdrawal, will never dare to attribute any good to himself, but will rather admit his poverty and emptiness. Give to God what is God's and ascribe to yourself what is yours. Give Him thanks, then, for His grace, but place upon yourself alone the blame and the punishment your fault deserves.

Always take the lowest place and the highest will be given you, for the highest cannot exist apart from the lowest. The saints who are greatest before God are those who consider themselves the least, and the more humble they are within themselves, so much the more glorious they are. Since they do not desire vainglory, they are full of truth and heavenly glory. Being established and strengthened in God, they can by no means be proud. They attribute to God whatever good they have received; they seek no glory from one another but only that which comes from God alone. They desire above all things that He be praised in themselves and in all His saints—this is their constant purpose.

Be grateful, therefore, for the least gift and you will be worthy to receive a greater. Consider the least gift as the greatest, the most contemptible as something special. And, if you but look to the dignity of the Giver, no gift will appear too small or worthless. Even though He give punishments and scourges, accept them, because He acts for our welfare in whatever He allows to befall us.

He who desires to keep the grace of God ought to be grateful when it is given and patient when it is withdrawn. Let him pray that it return; let him be cautious and humble lest he lose it.

The Eleventh Chapter

FEW LOVE THE CROSS OF JESUS

JESUS HAS always many who love His heavenly kingdom, but few who bear His cross. He has many who desire consolation, but few who care for trial. He finds many to share His table, but few to take part in His fasting. All desire to be happy with Him; few wish to suffer anything for Him. Many follow Him to the breaking of bread, but few to the drinking of the chalice of His passion. Many revere His miracles; few approach the shame of the Cross. Many love Him as long as they encounter no hardship; many praise and bless Him as long as they receive some comfort from Him. But if Jesus hides Himself and leaves them for a while, they fall either into complaints or into deep dejection. Those, on the contrary, who love Him for His own sake and not for any comfort of their own, bless Him in all trial and anguish of heart as well as in the bliss of consolation. Even if He should never give them consolation, yet they would continue to praise Him and wish always to give Him thanks. What power there is in pure love for Jesus—love that is free from all self-interest and self-love!

Do not those who always seek consolation deserve to be called mercenaries? Do not those who always think of their own profit and gain prove that they love themselves rather than Christ? Where can a man be found who desires to serve God for nothing? Rarely indeed is a man so spiritual as to strip himself of all things. And who shall find a man so truly poor in spirit as to be free from every creature? His value is like that of things brought from the most distant lands.

If a man give all his wealth, it is nothing; if he do great penance, it is little; if he gain all knowledge, he is still far afield; if he have great virtue and much ardent devotion, he still lacks a great deal, and especially, the one thing that is most necessary to him. What is this one thing? That leaving all, he forsake himself, completely renounce himself, and give up all private affections. Then, when he has done all that he knows ought to be done, let him consider it as nothing, let him make little of what may be considered great; let him in all honesty call himself an unprofitable servant. For truth itself has said: "When you shall have done all these things that are commanded you, say: 'we are unprofitable servants.'"[1]

Then he will be truly poor and stripped in spirit, and with the prophet may say: "I am alone and poor."[2] No one, however, is more wealthy than such a man; no one is more powerful, no one freer than he who knows how to leave all things and think of himself as the least of all.

The Twelfth Chapter

THE ROYAL ROAD OF THE HOLY CROSS

TO MANY the saying, "Deny thyself, take up thy cross and follow Me,"[1] seems hard, but it will be much harder to hear that final word: "Depart from Me, ye cursed, into everlasting fire."[2] Those who hear the word of

---

[1] Luke 17:10.
[2] Ps. 24:16.

---

[1] Matt. 16:24.
[2] Matt. 25:41.

the cross and follow it willingly now, need not fear that they will hear of eternal damnation on the day of judgment. This sign of the cross will be in the heavens when the Lord comes to judge. Then all the servants of the cross, who during life made themselves one with the Crucified, will draw near with great trust to Christ, the judge.

Why, then, do you fear to take up the cross when through it you can win a kingdom? In the cross is salvation, in the cross is life, in the cross is protection from enemies, in the cross is infusion of heavenly sweetness, in the cross is strength of mind, in the cross is joy of spirit, in the cross is highest virtue, in the cross is perfect holiness. There is no salvation of soul nor hope of everlasting life but in the cross.

Take up your cross, therefore, and follow Jesus, and you shall enter eternal life. He Himself opened the way before you in carrying His cross, and upon it He died for you, that you, too, might take up your cross and long to die upon it. If you die with Him, you shall also live with Him, and if you share His suffering, you shall also share His glory.

Behold, in the cross is everything, and upon your dying on the cross everything depends. There is no other way to life and to true inward peace than the way of the holy cross and daily mortification. Go where you will, seek what you will, you will not find a higher way, nor a less exalted but safer way, than the way of the holy cross. Arrange and order everything to suit your will and judgment, and still you will find that some suffering must always be borne, willingly or unwillingly, and thus you will always find the cross.

Either you will experience bodily pain or you will undergo tribulation of spirit in your soul. At times you will be forsaken by God, at times troubled by those about you and, what is worse, you will often grow weary of yourself. You cannot escape, you cannot be relieved by any remedy or comfort but must bear with it as long as God wills. For He wishes you to learn to bear trial without consolation, to submit yourself wholly to Him that you may become more humble through suffering. No one understands the passion of Christ so thoroughly or heartily as the man whose lot it is to suffer the like himself.

The cross, therefore, is always ready; it awaits you everywhere. No matter where you may go, you cannot escape it, for wherever you go you take yourself with you and shall always find yourself. Turn where you will—above, below, without, or within—you will find a cross in everything, and everywhere you must have patience if you would have peace within and merit an eternal crown.

If you carry the cross willingly, it will carry and lead you to the desired goal where indeed there shall be no more suffering, but here there shall be. If you carry it unwillingly, you create a burden for yourself and increase the load, though still you have to bear it. If you cast away one cross, you will find another and perhaps a heavier one. Do you expect to escape what no mortal man can ever avoid? Which of the saints was without a cross or trial on this earth? Not even Jesus Christ, our Lord, Whose every hour on earth knew the pain of His passion. "It behooveth Christ to suffer, and to rise again from the dead, . . . and so enter into his glory."[3] How is it that you look for another way than this, the royal way of the holy cross?

The whole life of Christ was a cross and a martyrdom, and do you seek rest and enjoyment for yourself? You deceive yourself, you are mistaken if you seek anything but to suffer, for this mortal life is full of miseries and marked with crosses on all sides. Indeed, the more spiritual progress a person makes, so much heavier will he frequently find the cross, because as his love increases, the pain of his exile also increases.

Yet such a man, though afflicted in many ways, is not without hope of consolation, because he knows that great reward is coming to him for bearing his cross. And when he carries it willingly, every pang of tribulation is changed into hope of solace from God. Besides, the more the flesh is distressed by affliction, so much the more is the spirit strengthened by inward grace. Not infrequently a man is so strengthened by his love of trials and hardship in his desire to conform to the cross of Christ, that he does not wish to be without sorrow or pain, since he believes he will be the more acceptable to God if he is able to endure more and more grievous things for His sake.

It is the grace of Christ, and not the virtue of man, which can and does bring it about that through fervor of spirit frail flesh learns to love and to gain what it naturally hates and shuns.

To carry the cross, to love the cross, to chastise the body and bring it to subjection, to flee honors, to endure contempt gladly, to despise self and wish to be despised, to suffer any adversity and loss, to desire no prosperous days on earth—this is not man's way. If you rely upon yourself, you can do none of these things, but if you trust in the Lord, strength will be given you from heaven and the world and the flesh will be made subject to your word. You will not even fear your enemy, the devil, if you are armed with faith and signed with the cross of Christ.

Set yourself, then, like a good and faithful servant of Christ, to bear manfully the cross of your Lord, Who out of love was crucified for you. Be ready to suffer many adversities and many kinds of trouble in this miserable life, for troublesome and miserable life will always be, no matter where you are; and so you will find it wherever you may hide. Thus it must be; and there is no way to evade the trials and sorrows of life but to bear them.

Drink the chalice of the Lord with affection if you wish to be His

---

[3] Luke 24:46, 26.

friend and to have part with Him. Leave consolation to God; let Him do as most pleases Him. On your part, be ready to bear sufferings and consider them the greatest consolation, for even though you alone were to undergo them all, the sufferings of this life are not worthy to be compared with the glory to come.

When you shall have come to the point where suffering is sweet and acceptable for the sake of Christ, then consider yourself fortunate, for you have found paradise on earth. But as long as suffering irks you and you seek to escape, so long will you be unfortunate, and the tribulation you seek to evade will follow you everywhere. If you put your mind to the things you ought to consider, that is, to suffering and death, you would soon be in a better state and would find peace.

Although you were taken to the third heaven with Paul, you were not thereby insured against suffering. Jesus said: "I will show him how great things he must suffer for My name's sake."[4] To suffer, then, remains your lot, if you mean to love Jesus and serve Him forever.

If you were but worthy to suffer something for the name of Jesus, what great glory would be in store for you, what great joy to all the saints of God, what great edification to those about you! For all men praise patience though there are few who wish to practice it.

With good reason, then, ought you to be willing to suffer a little for Christ since many suffer much more for the world.

Realize that you must lead a dying life; the more a man dies to himself, the more he begins to live unto God.

No man is fit to enjoy heaven unless he has resigned himself to suffer hardship for Christ. Nothing is more acceptable to God, nothing more helpful for you on this earth than to suffer willingly for Christ. If you had to make a choice, you ought to wish rather to suffer for Christ than to enjoy many consolations, for thus you would be more like Christ and more like all the saints. Our merit and progress consist not in many pleasures and comforts but rather in enduring great afflictions and sufferings.

If, indeed, there were anything better or more useful for man's salvation than suffering, Christ would have shown it by word and example. But He clearly exhorts the disciples who follow Him and all who wish to follow Him to carry the cross, saying: "If any man will come after Me, let him deny himself, and take up his cross daily, and follow Me."[5]

When, therefore, we have read and searched all that has been written, let this be the final conclusion—that through much suffering we must enter into the kingdom of God.

---

[4] Acts 9:16.
[5] Luke 9:23.

BOOK THREE

INTERNAL CONSOLATION

The First Chapter

THE INWARD CONVERSATION OF CHRIST
WITH THE FAITHFUL SOUL

I WILL hear what the Lord God will speak in me."[1]

Blessed is the soul who hears the Lord speaking within her, who receives the word of consolation from His lips. Blessed are the ears that catch the accents of divine whispering, and pay no heed to the murmurings of this world. Blessed indeed are the ears that listen, not to the voice which sounds without, but to the truth which teaches within. Blessed are the eyes which are closed to exterior things and are fixed upon those which are interior. Blessed are they who penetrate inwardly, who try daily to prepare themselves more and more to understand mysteries. Blessed are they who long to give their time to God, and who cut themselves off from the hindrances of the world.

Consider these things, my soul, and close the door of your senses, so that you can hear what the Lord your God speaks within you. "I am your salvation," says your Beloved. "I am your peace and your life. Remain with Me and you will find peace. Dismiss all passing things and seek the eternal. What are all temporal things but snares? And

---

[1] Ps. 84:9.

44

what help will all creatures be able to give you if you are deserted by the Creator?" Leave all these things, therefore, and make yourself pleasing and faithful to your Creator so that you may attain to true happiness.

The Second Chapter

TRUTH SPEAKS INWARDLY WITHOUT THE SOUND OF WORDS

THE DISCIPLE

"SPEAK, LORD, for Thy servant heareth."[1] "I am Thy servant. Give me understanding that I may know Thine ordinances[2] . . . Incline my heart to Thine ordinances[3] . . . Let Thy speech distil as the dew."[4]

The children of Israel once said to Moses: "Speak thou to us and we will hear thee: let not the Lord speak to us, lest we die."[5]

Not so, Lord, not so do I pray. Rather with Samuel the prophet I entreat humbly and earnestly: "Speak, Lord, for Thy servant heareth." Do not let Moses or any of the prophets speak to me; but You speak, O Lord God, Who inspired and enlightened all the prophets; for You alone, without them, can instruct me perfectly, whereas they, without You, can do nothing. They, indeed, utter fine words, but they cannot impart the spirit. They do indeed speak beautifully, but if You remain silent they cannot inflame the heart. They deliver the message; You lay bare the sense. They place before us mysteries, but You unlock their meaning. They proclaim commandments; You help us to keep them. They point out the way; You give strength for the journey. They work only outwardly; You instruct and enlighten our hearts. They water on the outside; You give the increase. They cry out words; You give understanding to the hearer.

Let not Moses speak to me, therefore, but You, the Lord my God, everlasting truth, speak lest I die and prove barren if I am merely given outward advice and am not inflamed within; lest the word heard and not kept, known and not loved, believed and not obeyed, rise up in judgment against me.

---

[1] I Kings 3:9.
[2] Ps. 118:125.
[3] Ps. 118:36.
[4] Deut. 32:2.
[5] Exod. 20:19.

Speak, therefore, Lord, for Your servant listens. "Thou hast the words of eternal life."[6] Speak to me for the comfort of my soul and for the amendment of my life, for Your praise, Your glory, and Your everlasting honor.

The Third Chapter

LISTEN HUMBLY TO THE WORDS OF GOD. MANY DO NOT HEED THEM

THE VOICE OF CHRIST

MY CHILD, hear My words, words of greatest sweetness surpassing all the knowledge of the philosophers and wise men of earth. My words are spirit and life, and they are not to be weighed by man's understanding. They are not to be invoked in vanity but are to be heard in silence, and accepted with all humility and with great affection.

THE DISCIPLE

"Happy is the man whom Thou admonishest, O Lord, and teachest out of Thy law, to give him peace from the days of evil,"[1] and that he be not desolate on earth.

THE VOICE OF CHRIST

I taught the prophets from the beginning, and even to this day I continue to speak to all men. But many are hardened. Many are deaf to My voice. Most men listen more willingly to the world than to God. They are more ready to follow the appetite of their flesh than the good pleasure of God. The world, which promises small and passing things, is served with great eagerness: I promise great and eternal things and the hearts of men grow dull. Who is there that serves and obeys Me in all things with as great care as that with which the world and its masters are served?

---

[6] John 6:69.

---

[1] Ps. 93:12.

"Be thou ashamed, O Sidon, for the sea speaketh."[2] And if you ask why, listen to the cause—for a small gain they travel far; for eternal life many will scarcely lift a foot from the ground. They seek a petty reward, and sometimes fight shamefully in law courts for a single piece of money. They are not afraid to work day and night for a trifle or an empty promise. But, for an unchanging good, for a reward beyond estimate, for the greatest honor and for glory everlasting, it must be said to their shame that men begrudge even the least fatigue. Be ashamed, then, lazy and complaining servant, that they should be found more eager for perdition than you are for life, that they rejoice more in vanity than you in truth.

Sometimes indeed their expectations fail them, but My promise never deceives, nor does it send away empty-handed him who trusts in Me. What I have promised I will give. What I have said I will fulfill, if only a man remain faithful in My love to the end. I am the rewarder of all the good, the strong approver of all who are devoted to Me.

Write My words in your heart and meditate on them earnestly, for in time of temptation they will be very necessary. What you do not understand when you read, you will learn in the day of visitation. I am wont to visit My elect in two ways—by temptation and by consolation. To them I read two lessons daily—one reproving their vices, the other exhorting them to progress in virtue. He who has My words and despises them has that which shall condemn him on the last day.

A PRAYER FOR THE GRACE OF DEVOTION

O Lord my God, You are all my good. And who am I that I should dare to speak to You? I am Your poorest and meanest servant, a vile worm, much more poor and contemptible than I know or dare to say. Yet remember me, Lord, because I am nothing, I have nothing, and I can do nothing. You alone are good, just, and holy. You can do all things, You give all things, You fill all things: only the sinner do You leave empty-handed. Remember Your tender mercies and fill my heart with Your grace, You Who will not allow Your works to be in vain. How can I bear this life of misery unless You comfort me with Your mercy and grace? Do not turn Your face from me. Do not delay Your visitation. Do not withdraw Your consolation, lest in Your sight my soul become as desert land. Teach me, Lord, to do Your will. Teach me to live worthily and humbly in Your sight, for You are my wisdom Who

---

[2] Isa. 23:4.

know me truly, and Who knew me even before the world was made and before I was born into it.

The Fourth Chapter

WE MUST WALK BEFORE GOD IN HUMILITY AND TRUTH

THE VOICE OF CHRIST

MY CHILD, walk before Me in truth, and seek Me always in the simplicity of your heart. He who walks before Me in truth shall be defended from the attacks of evil, and the truth shall free him from seducers and from the slanders of wicked men. For if the truth has made you free, then you shall be free indeed, and you shall not care for the vain words of men.

THE DISCIPLE

O Lord, it is true. I ask that it be with me as You say. Let your truth teach me. Let it guard me, and keep me safe to the end. Let it free me from all evil affection and badly ordered love, and I shall walk with You in great freedom of heart.

THE VOICE OF CHRIST

I shall teach you those things which are right and pleasing to Me. Consider your sins with great displeasure and sorrow, and never think yourself to be someone because of your good works. You are truly a sinner. You are subject to many passions and entangled in them. Of yourself you always tend to nothing. You fall quickly, are quickly overcome, quickly troubled, and quickly undone. You have nothing in which you can glory, but you have many things for which you should think yourself vile, for you are much weaker than you can comprehend. Hence, let none of the things you do seem great to you. Let nothing seem important or precious or desirable except that which is everlasting. Let the eternal truth please you above all things, and let your extreme unworthiness always displease you. Fear nothing, abhor nothing, and fly nothing as you do your own vices and sins; these should be more unpleasant for you than any material losses.

Some men walk before Me without sincerity. Led on by a certain curiosity and arrogance, they wish to know My secrets and to understand the high things of God, to the neglect of themselves and their own salvation. Through their own pride and curiosity, and because I am against them, such men often fall into great temptations and sins.

Fear the judgments of God! Dread the wrath of the Almighty! Do not discuss the works of the Most High, but examine your sins—in what serious things you have offended and how many good things you have neglected.

Some carry their devotion only in books, some in pictures, some in outward signs and figures. Some have Me on their lips when there is little of Me in their hearts. Others, indeed, with enlightened understanding and purified affections, constantly long for everlasting things; they are unwilling to hear of earthly affairs and only with reluctance do they serve the necessities of nature. These sense what the Spirit of truth speaks within them: for He teaches them to despise earthly things and to love those of heaven, to neglect the world, and each day and night to desire heaven.

The Fifth Chapter

THE WONDERFUL EFFECT OF DIVINE LOVE

THE DISCIPLE

I BLESS You, O heavenly Father, Father of my Lord Jesus Christ, for having condescended to remember me, a poor creature. Thanks to You, O Father of mercies, God of all consolation, Who with Your comfort sometimes refresh me, who am not worthy of it. I bless You always and glorify You with Your only-begotten Son and the Holy Spirit, the Paraclete, forever and ever.

Ah, Lord God, my holy Lover, when You come into my heart, all that is within me will rejoice. You are my glory and the exultation of my heart. You are my hope and refuge in the day of my tribulation. But because my love is as yet weak and my virtue imperfect, I must be strengthened and comforted by You. Visit me often, therefore, and teach me Your holy discipline. Free me from evil passions and cleanse my heart of all disorderly affection so that, healed and purified within, I may be fit to love, strong to suffer, and firm to persevere.

Love is an excellent thing, a very great blessing, indeed. It makes every difficulty easy, and bears all wrongs with equanimity. For it bears a burden without being weighted and renders sweet all that is bitter. The noble love of Jesus spurs to great deeds and excites longing for that which is more perfect. Love tends upward; it will not be held down by anything low. Love wishes to be free and estranged from all worldly affections, lest its inward sight be obstructed, lest it be entangled in any temporal interest and overcome by adversity.

Nothing is sweeter than love, nothing stronger or higher or wider; nothing is more pleasant, nothing fuller, and nothing better in heaven or on earth, for love is born of God and cannot rest except in God, Who is above all created things.

One who is in love flies, runs, and rejoices; he is free, not bound. He gives all for all and possesses all in all, because he rests in the one sovereign Good, Who is above all things, and from Whom every good flows and proceeds. He does not look to the gift but turns himself above all gifts to the Giver.

Love often knows no limits but overflows all bounds. Love feels no burden, thinks nothing of troubles, attempts more than it is able, and does not plead impossibility, because it believes that it may and can do all things. For this reason, it is able to do all, performing and effecting much where he who does not love fails and falls.

Love is watchful. Sleeping, it does not slumber. Wearied, it is not tired. Pressed, it is not straitened. Alarmed, it is not confused, but like a living flame, a burning torch, it forces its way upward and passes unharmed through every obstacle.

If a man loves, he will know the sound of this voice. For this warm affection of soul is a loud voice crying in the ears of God, and it says: "My God, my love, You are all mine and I am all Yours. Give me an increase of love, that I may learn to taste with the inward lips of my heart how sweet it is to love, how sweet to be dissolved in love and bathe in it. Let me be rapt in love. Let me rise above self in great fervor and wonder. Let me sing the hymn of love, and let me follow You, my Love, to the heights. Let my soul exhaust itself in praising You, rejoicing out of love. Let me love You more than myself, and let me not love myself except for Your sake. In You let me love all those who truly love You, as the law of love, which shines forth from You, commands."

Love is swift, sincere, kind, pleasant, and delightful. Love is strong, patient and faithful, prudent, long-suffering, and manly. Love is never self-seeking, for in whatever a person seeks himself there he falls from love. Love is circumspect, humble, and upright. It is neither soft nor light, nor intent upon vain things. It is sober and chaste, firm and quiet, guarded in all the senses. Love is subject and obedient to superiors. It is mean and contemptible in its own eyes, devoted and thankful to God; always trusting and hoping in Him even when He is distasteful to it, for there is no living in love without sorrow. He who is not ready to suffer all things and to stand resigned to the will of the Beloved is not worthy to be called a lover. A lover must embrace willingly all that is difficult and bitter for the sake of the Beloved, and he should not turn away from Him because of adversities.

The Sixth Chapter

THE PROVING OF A TRUE LOVER

THE VOICE OF CHRIST

MY CHILD, you are not yet a brave and wise lover.

THE DISCIPLE

Why, Lord?

THE VOICE OF CHRIST

Because, on account of a slight difficulty you give up what you have undertaken and are too eager to seek consolation.

The brave lover stands firm in temptations and pays no heed to the crafty persuasions of the enemy. As I please him in prosperity, so in adversity I am not displeasing to him. The wise lover regards not so much the gift of Him Who loves as the love of Him Who gives. He regards the affection of the Giver rather than the value of the gift, and sets his Beloved above all gifts. The noble lover does not rest in the gift but in Me Who am above every gift.

All is not lost, then, if you sometimes feel less devout than you wish toward Me or My saints. That good and sweet feeling which you sometimes have is the effect of present grace and a certain foretaste of your heavenly home. You must not lean upon it too much, because it comes and goes. But to fight against evil thoughts which attack you is a sign of virtue and great merit. Do not, therefore, let strange fantasies disturb you, no matter what they concern. Hold strongly to your resolution and keep a right intention toward God.

It is not an illusion that you are sometimes rapt in ecstasy and then quickly returned to the usual follies of your heart. For these are evils which you suffer rather than commit; and so long as they displease you and you struggle against them, it is a matter of merit and not a loss.

You must know that the old enemy tries by all means in his power to hinder your desire for good and to turn you from every devotional practice, especially from the veneration of the saints, from devout meditation on My passion, and from your firm purpose of advancing in virtue. He suggests many evil thoughts that he may cause you weariness and horror, and thus draw you away from prayer and holy reading. A humble confession displeases him and, if he could, he would make you omit Holy Communion.

Do not believe him or heed him, even though he often sets traps to deceive you. When he suggests evil, unclean things, accuse him. Say to him: "Away, unclean spirit! Shame, miserable creature! You are but filth to bring such things to my ears. Begone, most wretched seducer! You shall have no part in me, for Jesus will be my strength, and you shall be confounded. I would rather die and suffer all torments than consent to you. Be still! Be silent! Though you bring many troubles upon me I will have none of you. The Lord is my light, my salvation. Whom shall I fear? Though armies unite against me, my heart will not fear, for the Lord is my Helper, my Redeemer."

Fight like a good soldier and if you sometimes fall through weakness, rise again with greater strength than before, trusting in My most abundant grace. But beware of vain complacency and pride. For many are led into error through these faults and sometimes fall into almost perpetual blindness. Let the fall of these, who proudly presume on self, be a warning to you and a constant incentive to humility.

The Seventh Chapter

GRACE MUST BE HIDDEN UNDER THE MANTLE OF HUMILITY

THE VOICE OF CHRIST

IT IS better and safer for you to conceal the grace of devotion, not to be elated by it, not to speak or think much of it, and instead to humble yourself and fear lest it is being given to one unworthy of it. Do not cling too closely to this affection, for it may quickly be changed to its opposite. When you are in grace, think how miserable and needy you are without it. Your progress in spiritual life does not consist in having the grace of consolation, but in enduring its withdrawal with humility, resignation, and patience, so that you neither become listless in prayer nor neglect your other duties in the least; but on the contrary do what you can do as well as you know how, and do not neglect yourself completely because of your dryness or anxiety of mind.

There are many, indeed, who immediately become impatient and lazy when things do not go well with them. The way of man, however, does not always lie in his own power. It is God's prerogative to give grace and to console when He wishes, as much as He wishes, and whom He wishes, as it shall please Him and no more.

Some careless persons, misusing the grace of devotion, have destroyed themselves because they wished to do more than they were able. They failed to take account of their own weakness, and followed the desire of their heart rather than the judgment of their reason. Then, because they presumed to greater things than pleased God they quickly lost His grace. They who had built their homes in heaven became helpless, vile outcasts, humbled and impoverished, that they might learn not to fly with their own wings but to trust in Mine.

They who are still new and inexperienced in the way of the Lord may easily be deceived and overthrown unless they guide themselves by the advice of discreet persons. But if they wish to follow their own notions rather than to trust in others who are more experienced, they will be in danger of a sorry end, at least if they are unwilling to be drawn from their vanity. Seldom do they who are wise in their own conceits bear humbly the guidance of others. Yet a little knowledge humbly and meekly pursued is better than great treasures of learning sought in vain complacency. It is better for you to have little than to have much which may become the source of pride.

He who gives himself up entirely to enjoyment acts very unwisely, for he forgets his former helplessness and that chastened fear of the Lord which dreads to lose a proffered grace. Nor is he very brave or wise who becomes too despondent in times of adversity and difficulty and thinks less confidently of Me than he should. He who wishes to be too secure in time of peace will often become too dejected and fearful in time of trial.

If you were wise enough to remain always humble and small in your own eyes, and to restrain and rule your spirit well, you would not fall so quickly into danger and offense.

When a spirit of fervor is enkindled within you, you may well meditate on how you will feel when the fervor leaves. Then, when this happens, remember that the light which I have withdrawn for a time as a warning to you and for My own glory may again return. Such trials are often more beneficial than if you had things always as you wish. For a man's merits are not measured by many visions or consolations, or by knowledge of the Scriptures, or by his being in a higher position than others, but by the truth of his humility, by his capacity for divine charity, by his constancy in seeking purely and entirely the honor of God, by his disregard and positive contempt of self, and more, by preferring to be despised and humiliated rather than honored by others.

The Eighth Chapter

SELF-ABASEMENT IN THE SIGHT OF GOD

THE DISCIPLE

I WILL speak to my Lord, I who am but dust and ashes. If I consider myself anything more than this, behold You stand against me, and my sins bear witness to the truth which I cannot contradict. If I abase myself, however, if I humble myself to nothingness, if I shrink from all self-esteem and account myself as the dust which I am, Your grace will favor me, Your light will enshroud my heart, and all self-esteem, no matter how little, will sink in the depths of my nothingness to perish forever.

It is there You show me to myself—what I am, what I have been, and what I am coming to; for I am nothing and I did not know it. Left to myself, I am nothing but total weakness. But if You look upon me for an instant, I am at once made strong and filled with new joy. Great wonder it is that I, who of my own weight always sink to the depths, am so suddenly lifted up, and so graciously embraced by You.

It is Your love that does this, graciously upholding me, supporting me in so many necessities, guarding me from so many grave dangers, and snatching me, as I may truly say, from evils without number. Indeed, by loving myself badly I lost myself; by seeking only You and by truly loving You I have found both myself and You, and by that love I have reduced myself more profoundly to nothing. For You, O sweetest Lord, deal with me above all my merits and above all that I dare to hope or ask.

May You be blessed, my God, for although I am unworthy of any benefits, yet Your nobility and infinite goodness never cease to do good even for those who are ungrateful and far from You. Convert us to You, that we may be thankful, humble, and devout, for You are our salvation, our courage, and our strength.

The Ninth Chapter

ALL THINGS SHOULD BE REFERRED
TO GOD AS THEIR LAST END

THE VOICE OF CHRIST

MY CHILD, I must be your supreme and last end, if you truly desire to be blessed. With this intention your affections, which are too often perversely inclined to self and to creatures, will be purified. For if you seek yourself in anything, you immediately fail interiorly and become dry of heart.

Refer all things principally to Me, therefore, for it is I Who have given them all. Consider each thing as flowing from the highest good, and therefore to Me, as to their highest source, must all things be brought back.

From Me the small and the great, the poor and the rich draw the water of life as from a living fountain, and they who serve Me willingly and freely shall receive grace upon grace. He who wishes to glory in things apart from Me, however, or to delight in some good as his own, shall not be grounded in true joy or gladdened in his heart, but shall be burdened and distressed in many ways. Hence you ought not to attribute any good to yourself or ascribe virtue to any man, but give all to God without Whom man has nothing.

I have given all things. I will that all be returned to Me again, and I exact most strictly a return of thanks. This is the truth by which vainglory is put to flight.

Where heavenly grace and true charity enter in, there neither envy nor narrowness of heart nor self-love will have place. Divine love conquers all and enlarges the powers of the soul.

If you are truly wise, you will rejoice only in Me, because no one is good except God alone, Who is to be praised above all things and above all to be blessed.

The Tenth Chapter

TO DESPISE THE WORLD AND SERVE GOD IS SWEET

The Disciple

Now again I will speak, Lord, and will not be silent. I will speak to the hearing of my God, my Lord, and my King Who is in heaven. How great, O Lord, is the multitude of Your mercies which You have stored up for those who love You. But what are You to those who love You? What are You to those who serve You with their whole heart?

Truly beyond the power of words is the sweetness of contemplation You give to those who love You. To me You have shown the sweetness of Your charity, especially in having made me when I did not exist, in having brought me back to serve You when I had gone far astray from You, in having commanded me to love You.

O Fountain of unceasing love, what shall I say of You? How can I forget You, Who have been pleased to remember me even after I had wasted away and perished? You have shown mercy to Your servant beyond all hope, and have exhibited grace and friendship beyond his deserving.

What return shall I make to You for this grace? For it is not given every man to forsake all things, to renounce the world, and undertake the religious life. Is it anything great that I should serve You Whom every creature is bound to serve? It should not seem much to me; instead it should appear great and wonderful that You condescend to receive into Your service one who is so poor and unworthy. Behold, all things are Yours, even those which I have and by which I serve You. Behold, heaven and earth which You created for the service of man, stand ready, and each day they do whatever You command. But even this is little, for You have appointed angels also to minister to man—yea more than all this—You Yourself have condescended to serve man and have promised to give him Yourself.

What return shall I make for all these thousands of benefits? Would that I could serve You all the days of my life! Would that for but one day I could serve You worthily! Truly You are worthy of all service, all honor, and everlasting praise. Truly You are my Lord, and I am Your poor servant, bound to serve You with all my powers, praising You without ever becoming weary. I wish to do this—this is my desire. Do You supply whatever is wanting in me.

It is a great honor, a great glory to serve You and to despise all things for Your sake. They who give themselves gladly to Your most holy service will possess great grace. They who cast aside all carnal delights for Your love will find the most sweet consolation of the Holy Ghost. They who enter upon the narrow way for Your name and cast aside all worldly care will attain great freedom of mind.

O sweet and joyful service of God, which makes man truly free and holy! O sacred state of religious bondage which makes man equal to the angels, pleasing to God, terrible to the demons, and worthy of the commendation of all the faithful! O service to be embraced and always desired, in which the highest good is offered and joy is won which shall remain forever!

The Eleventh Chapter

THE LONGINGS OF OUR HEARTS MUST BE EXAMINED AND MODERATED

THE VOICE OF CHRIST

MY CHILD, it is necessary for you to learn many things which you have not yet learned well.

THE DISCIPLE

What are they, Lord?

THE VOICE OF CHRIST

That you conform your desires entirely according to My good pleasure, and be not a lover of self but an earnest doer of My will. Desires very often inflame you and drive you madly on, but consider whether you act for My honor, or for your own advantage. If I am the cause, you will be well content with whatever I ordain. If, on the other hand, any self-seeking lurk in you, it troubles you and weighs you down. Take care, then, that you do not rely too much on preconceived desire that has no reference to Me, lest you repent later on and be displeased with what at first pleased you and which you desired as being for the best. Not every desire which seems good should be followed immediately, nor, on the other hand, should every contrary affection be at once rejected.

It is sometimes well to use a little restraint even in good desires and inclinations, lest through too much eagerness you bring upon yourself distraction of mind; lest through your lack of discipline you create scandal for others; or lest you be suddenly upset and fall because of resistance from others. Sometimes, however, you must use violence and resist your sensual appetite manfully. You must pay no attention to what the flesh does or does not desire, taking pains that it be subjected, even by force, to the spirit. And it should be chastised and forced to remain in subjection until it is prepared for anything and is taught to be satisfied with little, to take pleasure in simple things, and not to murmur against inconveniences.

The Twelfth Chapter

ACQUIRING PATIENCE IN THE FIGHT AGAINST CONCUPISCENCE

THE DISCIPLE

PATIENCE, O Lord God, is very necessary for me, I see, because there are many adversities in this life. No matter what plans I make for my own peace, my life cannot be free from struggle and sorrow.

The Voice of Christ

My child, you are right, yet My wish is not that you seek that peace which is free from temptations or meets with no opposition, but rather that you consider yourself as having found peace when you have been tormented with many tribulations and tried with many adversities.

If you say that you cannot suffer much, how will you endure the fire of purgatory? Of two evils, the lesser is always to be chosen. Therefore, in order that you may escape the everlasting punishments to come, try to bear present evils patiently for the sake of God.

Do you think that men of the world have no suffering, or perhaps but little? Ask even those who enjoy the most delights and you will learn otherwise. "But," you will say, "they enjoy many pleasures and follow their own wishes; therefore they do not feel their troubles very much." Granted that they do have whatever they wish, how long do you think it will last? Behold, they who prosper in the world shall perish as smoke, and there shall be no memory of their past joys. Even in this life they do not find rest in these pleasures without bitterness, weariness, and fear. For they often receive the penalty of sorrow from the very thing whence they believe their happiness comes. And it is just. Since they seek and follow after pleasures without reason, they should not enjoy them without shame and bitterness.

How brief, how false, how unreasonable and shameful all these pleasures are! Yet in their drunken blindness men do not understand this, but like brute beasts incur death of soul for the miserly enjoyment of a corruptible life.

Therefore, My child, do not pursue your lusts, but turn away from your own will. "Seek thy pleasure in the Lord and He will give thee thy heart's desires."[1] If you wish to be truly delighted and more abundantly comforted by Me, behold, in contempt of all worldly things and in the cutting off of all base pleasures shall your blessing be, and great consolation shall be given you. Further, the more you withdraw yourself from any solace of creatures, the sweeter and stronger comfort will you find in Me.

At first you will not gain these blessings without sadness and toil and conflict. Habit already formed will resist you, but it shall be overcome by a better habit. The flesh will murmur against you, but it will be bridled by fervor of spirit. The old serpent will sting and trouble you, but prayer will put him to flight and by steadfast, useful toil the way will be closed to him.

---

[1] Ps. 37:4.

The Thirteenth Chapter

THE OBEDIENCE OF ONE HUMBLY SUBJECT TO THE EXAMPLE OF JESUS CHRIST

THE VOICE OF CHRIST

MY CHILD, he who attempts to escape obeying withdraws himself from grace. Likewise he who seeks private benefits for himself loses those which are common to all. He who does not submit himself freely and willingly to his superior, shows that his flesh is not yet perfectly obedient but that it often rebels and murmurs against him.

Learn quickly, then, to submit yourself to your superior if you wish to conquer your own flesh. For the exterior enemy is more quickly overcome if the inner man is not laid waste. There is no more troublesome, no worse enemy of the soul than you yourself, if you are not in harmony with the spirit. It is absolutely necessary that you conceive a true contempt for yourself if you wish to be victorious over flesh and blood.

Because you still love yourself too inordinately, you are afraid to resign yourself wholly to the will of others. Is it such a great matter if you, who are but dust and nothingness, subject yourself to man for the sake of God, when I, the All-Powerful, the Most High, Who created all things out of nothing, humbly subjected Myself to man for your sake? I became the most humble and the lowest of all men that you might overcome your pride with My humility.

Learn to obey, you who are but dust! Learn to humble yourself, you who are but earth and clay, and bow down under the foot of every man! Learn to break your own will, to submit to all subjection! Be zealous against yourself! Allow no pride to dwell in you, but prove yourself so humble and lowly that all may walk over you and trample upon you as dust in the streets!

What have you, vain man, to complain of? What answer can you make, vile sinner, to those who accuse you, you who have so often offended God and so many times deserved hell? But My eye has spared you because your soul was precious in My sight, so that you might know My love and always be thankful for My benefits, so that you might give yourself continually to true subjection and humility, and might patiently endure contempt.

The Fourteenth Chapter

CONSIDER THE HIDDEN JUDGMENTS OF GOD LEST YOU BECOME PROUD OF YOUR OWN GOOD DEEDS

THE DISCIPLE

YOU THUNDER forth Your judgments over me, Lord. You shake all my bones with fear and trembling, and my soul is very much afraid. I stand in awe as I consider that the heavens are not pure in Your sight. If You found wickedness in the angels and did not spare them, what will become of me? Stars have fallen from heaven, and I—I who am but dust—how can I be presumptuous? They whose deeds seemed worthy of praise have fallen into the depths, and I have seen those who ate the bread of angels delighting themselves with the husks of swine.

There is no holiness, then, if You withdraw Your hand, Lord. There is no wisdom if You cease to guide, no courage if You cease to defend. No chastity is secure if You do not guard it. Our vigilance avails nothing if Your holy watchfulness does not protect us. Left to ourselves we sink and perish, but visited by You we are lifted up and live. We are truly unstable, but You make us strong. We grow lukewarm, but You inflame us.

Oh, how humbly and lowly should I consider myself! How very little should I esteem anything that seems good in me! How profoundly should I submit to Your unfathomable judgments, Lord, where I find myself to be but nothing!

O immeasurable weight! O impassable sea, where I find myself to be nothing but bare nothingness! Where, then, is glory's hiding place? Where can there be any trust in my own virtue? All vainglory is swallowed up in the depths of Your judgments upon me.

What is all flesh in Your sight? Shall the clay glory against Him that formed it? How can he whose heart is truly subject to God be lifted up by vainglory? The whole world will not make him proud whom truth has subjected to itself. Nor shall he who has placed all his hope in God be moved by the tongues of flatterers. For behold, even they who speak are nothing; they will pass away with the sound of their words, but the truth of the Lord remains forever.

The Fifteenth Chapter

HOW ONE SHOULD FEEL AND SPEAK ON EVERY DESIRABLE THING

THE VOICE OF CHRIST

My child, this is the way you must speak on every occasion: "Lord, if it be pleasing to You, so be it. If it be to Your honor, Lord, be it done in Your name. Lord, if You see that it is expedient and profitable for me, then grant that I may use it to Your honor. But if You know that it will be harmful to me, and of no good benefit to the welfare of my soul, then take this desire away from me."

Not every desire is from the Holy Spirit, even though it may seem right and good. It is difficult to be certain whether it is a good spirit or a bad one that prompts one to this or that, and even to know whether you are being moved by your own spirit. Many who seemed at first to be led by a good spirit have been deceived in the end.

Whatever the mind sees as good, ask and desire in fear of God and humility of heart. Above all, commit the whole matter to Me with true resignation, and say: "Lord, You know what is better for me; let this be done or that be done as You please. Grant what You will, as much as You will, when You will. Do with me as You know best, as will most please You, and will be for Your greater honor. Place me where You will and deal with me freely in all things. I am in Your hand; turn me about whichever way You will. Behold, I am Your servant, ready to obey in all things. Not for myself do I desire to live, but for You—would that I could do this worthily and perfectly!"

A PRAYER THAT THE WILL OF GOD BE DONE

Grant me Your grace, O most merciful Jesus, that it may be with me, and work with me, and remain with me to the very end. Grant that I may always desire and will that which is most acceptable and pleasing to You. Let Your will be mine. Let my will always follow Yours and agree perfectly with it. Let my will be one with Yours in willing and in not willing, and let me be unable to will or not will anything but what You will or do not will. Grant that I may die to all things in this world, and for Your sake love to be despised and unknown in this life. Give me above all desires the desire to rest in You, and in You let my heart have peace. You are true peace of heart. You alone are its rest. Without You all things are difficult and troubled. In this peace, the selfsame that is in You, the Most High, the everlasting Good, I will sleep and take my rest. Amen.

The Sixteenth Chapter

TRUE COMFORT IS TO BE SOUGHT IN GOD ALONE

THE DISCIPLE

WHATEVER I can desire or imagine for my own comfort I look for not here but hereafter. For if I alone should have all the world's comforts and could enjoy all its delights, it is certain that they could not long endure. Therefore, my soul, you cannot enjoy full consolation or perfect delight except in God, the Consoler of the poor and the Helper of the humble. Wait a little, my soul, wait for the divine promise and you will have an abundance of all good things in heaven. If you desire these present things too much, you will lose those which are everlasting and heavenly. Use temporal things but desire eternal things. You cannot be satisfied with any temporal goods because you were not created to enjoy them.

Even if you possessed all created things you could not be happy and blessed; for in God, Who created all these things, your whole blessedness and happiness consists — not indeed such happiness as is seen and praised by lovers of the world, but such as that for which the good and faithful servants of Christ wait, and of which the spiritual and pure of heart, whose conversation is in heaven, sometime have a foretaste.

Vain and brief is all human consolation. But that which is received inwardly from the Truth is blessed and true. The devout man carries his Consoler, Jesus, everywhere with him, and he says to Him: "Be with me, Lord Jesus, in every place and at all times. Let this be my consolation, to be willing to forego all human comforting. And if Your consolation be wanting to me, let Your will and just trial of me be my greatest comfort. For You will not always be angry, nor will You threaten forever."

The Seventeenth Chapter

ALL OUR CARE IS TO BE PLACED IN GOD

The Voice of Christ

My child, allow me to do what I will with you. I know what is best for you. You think as a man; you feel in many things as human affection persuades.

The Disciple

Lord, what You say is true. Your care for me is greater than all the care I can take of myself. For he who does not cast all his care upon You stands very unsafely. If only my will remain right and firm toward You, Lord, do with me whatever pleases You. For whatever You shall do with me can only be good.

If You wish me to be in darkness, I shall bless You. And if You wish me to be in light, again I shall bless You. If You stoop down to comfort me, I shall bless You, and if You wish me to be afflicted, I shall bless You forever.

The Voice of Christ

My child, this is the disposition which you should have if you wish to walk with Me. You should be as ready to suffer as to enjoy. You should as willingly be destitute and poor as rich and satisfied.

The Disciple

O Lord, I shall suffer willingly for Your sake whatever You wish to send me. I am ready to accept from Your hand both good and evil alike, the sweet and the bitter together, sorrow with joy; and for all that happens to me I am grateful. Keep me from all sin and I will fear neither death nor hell. Do not cast me out forever nor blot me out of the Book of Life, and whatever tribulation befalls will not harm me.

The Eighteenth Chapter

TEMPORAL SUFFERINGS SHOULD BE BORNE PATIENTLY, AFTER THE EXAMPLE OF CHRIST

THE VOICE OF CHRIST

MY CHILD, I came down from heaven for your salvation and took upon Myself your miseries, not out of necessity but out of love, that you might learn to be patient and bear the sufferings of this life without repining. From the moment of My birth to My death on the cross, suffering did not leave Me. I suffered great want of temporal goods. Often I heard many complaints against Me. Disgrace and reviling I bore with patience. For My blessings I received ingratitude, for My miracles blasphemies, and for My teaching scorn.

THE DISCIPLE

O Lord, because You were patient in life, especially in fulfilling the design of the Father, it is fitting that I, a most miserable sinner, should live patiently according to Your will, and, as long as You shall wish, bear the burden of this corruptible body for the welfare of my soul. For though this present life seems burdensome, yet by Your grace it becomes meritorious, and it is made brighter and more endurable for the weak by Your example and the pathways of the saints. But it has also more consolation than formerly under the old law when the gates of heaven were closed, when the way thereto seemed darker than now, and when so few cared to seek the eternal kingdom. The just, the elect, could not enter heaven before Your sufferings and sacred death had paid the debt.

Oh, what great thanks I owe You, Who have shown me and all the faithful the good and right way to Your everlasting kingdom! Your life is our way and in Your holy patience we come nearer to You Who are our crown. Had You not gone before and taught us, who would have cared to follow? Alas, how many would have remained far behind, had they not before their eyes Your holy example! Behold, even we who have heard of Your many miracles and teachings are still lukewarm; what would happen if we did not have such light by which to follow You?

The Nineteenth Chapter

TRUE PATIENCE IN SUFFERING

The Voice of Christ

WHAT ARE you saying, My child? Think of My suffering and that of the saints, and cease complaining. You have not yet resisted to the shedding of blood. What you suffer is very little compared with the great things they suffered who were so strongly tempted, so severely troubled, so tried and tormented in many ways. Well may you remember, therefore, the very painful woes of others, that you may bear your own little ones the more easily. And if they do not seem so small to you, examine if perhaps your impatience is not the cause of their apparent greatness; and whether they are great or small, try to bear them all patiently. The better you dispose yourself to suffer, the more wisely you act and the greater is the reward promised you. Thus you will suffer more easily if your mind and habits are diligently trained to it.

Do not say: "I cannot bear this from such a man, nor should I suffer things of this kind, for he has done me a great wrong. He has accused me of many things of which I never thought. However, from someone else I will gladly suffer as much as I think I should."

Such a thought is foolish, for it does not consider the virtue of patience or the One Who will reward it, but rather weighs the person and the offense committed. The man who will suffer only as much as seems good to him, who will accept suffering only from those from whom he is pleased to accept it, is not truly patient. For the truly patient man does not consider from whom the suffering comes, whether from a superior, an equal, or an inferior, whether from a good and holy person or from a perverse and unworthy one; but no matter how great an adversity befalls him, no matter how often it comes or from whom it comes, he accepts it gratefully from the hand of God, and counts it a great gain. For with God nothing that is suffered for His sake, no matter how small, can pass without reward. Be prepared for the fight, then, if you wish to gain the victory. Without struggle you cannot obtain the crown of patience, and if you refuse to suffer you are refusing the crown. But if you desire to be crowned, fight manfully and bear up patiently. Without labor there is no rest, and without fighting, no victory.

THE DISCIPLE

O Lord, let that which seems naturally impossible to me become possible through Your grace. You know that I can suffer very little, and that I am quickly discouraged when any small adversity arises. Let the torment of tribulation suffered for Your name be pleasant and desirable to me, since to suffer and be troubled for Your sake is very beneficial for my soul.

The Twentieth Chapter

CONFESSING OUR WEAKNESS IN THE MISERIES OF LIFE

THE DISCIPLE

I WILL bring witness against myself to my injustice, and to You, O Lord, I will confess my weakness.

Often it is a small thing that makes me downcast and sad. I propose to act bravely, but when even a small temptation comes I find myself in great straits. Sometimes it is the merest trifle which gives rise to grievous temptations. When I think myself somewhat safe and when I am not expecting it, I frequently find myself almost overcome by a slight wind. Look, therefore, Lord, at my lowliness and frailty which You know so well. Have mercy on me and snatch me out of the mire that I may not be caught in it and may not remain forever utterly despondent.

That I am so prone to fall and so weak in resisting my passions oppresses me frequently and confounds me in Your sight. While I do not fully consent to them, still their assault is very troublesome and grievous to me, and it wearies me exceedingly thus to live in daily strife. Yet from the fact that abominable fancies rush in upon me much more easily than they leave, my weakness becomes clear to me.

Oh that You, most mighty God of Israel, zealous Lover of faithful souls, would consider the labor and sorrow of Your servant, and assist him in all his undertakings! Strengthen me with heavenly courage lest the outer man, the miserable flesh, against which I shall be obliged to fight so long as I draw a breath in this wretched life and which is not yet subjected to the spirit, prevail and dominate me.

Alas! What sort of life is this, from which troubles and miseries are never absent, where all things are full of snares and enemies? For when one trouble or temptation leaves, another comes. Indeed, even while the first conflict is still raging, many others begin unexpectedly. How is it possible to love a life that has such great bitterness, that is subject to so many calamities and miseries? Indeed, how can it even be called life when it begets so many deaths and plagues? And yet, it is loved, and many seek their delight in it.

Many persons often blame the world for being false and vain, yet do not readily give it up because the desires of the flesh have such great power. Some things draw them to love the world, others make them despise it. The lust of the flesh, the desire of the eyes, and the pride of life lead to love, while the pains and miseries, which are the just consequences of those things, beget hatred and weariness of the world.

Vicious pleasure overcomes the soul that is given to the world. She thinks that there are delights beneath these thorns, because she has never seen or tasted the sweetness of God or the internal delight of virtue. They, on the other hand, who entirely despise the world and seek to live for God under the rule of holy discipline, are not ignorant of the divine sweetness promised to those who truly renounce the world. They see clearly how gravely the world errs, and in how many ways it deceives.

The Twenty-First Chapter

ABOVE ALL GOODS AND ALL GIFTS WE MUST REST IN GOD

THE DISCIPLE

ABOVE ALL things and in all things, O my soul, rest always in God, for He is the everlasting rest of the saints.

Grant, most sweet and loving Jesus, that I may seek my repose in You above every creature; above all health and beauty; above every honor and glory; every power and dignity; above all knowledge and cleverness, all riches and arts, all joy and gladness; above all fame and praise, all sweetness and consolation; above every hope and promise, every merit and desire; above all the gifts and favors that You can give or pour down upon me; above all the joy and exultation that the mind can receive and feel; and finally, above the angels and archangels and all the heavenly host; above all things visible and invisible; and may I seek my repose in You above everything that is not You, my God.

For You, O Lord my God, are above all things the best. You alone are most high, You alone most powerful. You alone are most sufficient and most satisfying, You alone most sweet and consoling. You alone are most beautiful and loving, You alone most noble and glorious above all things. In You is every perfection that has been or ever will be. Therefore, whatever You give me besides Yourself, whatever You reveal to me concerning Yourself, and whatever You promise, is too small and insufficient when I do not see and fully enjoy You alone. For my heart cannot rest or be fully content until, rising above all gifts and every created thing, it rests in You.

Who, O most beloved Spouse, Jesus Christ, most pure Lover, Lord of all creation, who shall give me the wings of true liberty that I may fly to rest in You? When shall freedom be fully given me to see how sweet You are, O Lord, my God? When shall I recollect myself entirely in You, so that because of Your love I may feel, not myself, but You alone above all sense and measure, in a manner known to none? But now I often lament and grieve over my unhappiness, for many evils befall me in this vale of miseries, often disturbing me, making me sad and overshadowing me, often hindering and distracting me, alluring and entangling me so that I neither have free access to You nor enjoy the sweet embraces which are ever ready for blessed souls. Let my sighs and the manifold desolation here on earth move You.

O Jesus, Splendor of eternal glory, Consolation of the pilgrim soul, with You my lips utter no sound and to You my silence speaks. How long will my Lord delay His coming? Let Him come to His poor servant and make him happy. Let Him put forth His hand and take this miserable creature from his anguish. Come, O come, for without You there will be no happy day or hour, because You are my happiness and without You my table is empty. I am wretched, as it were imprisoned and weighted down with fetters, until You fill me with the light of Your presence, restore me to liberty, and show me a friendly countenance. Let others seek instead of You whatever they will, but nothing pleases me or will please me but You, my God, my Hope, my everlasting Salvation. I will not be silent, I will not cease praying until Your grace returns to me and You speak inwardly to me, saying: "Behold, I am here. Lo, I have come to you because you have called Me. Your tears and the desire of your soul, your humility and contrition of heart have inclined Me and brought Me to you."

Lord, I have called You, and have desired You, and have been ready to spurn all things for Your sake. For You first spurred me on to seek You. May You be blessed, therefore, O Lord, for having shown this goodness to Your servant according to the multitude of Your mercies.

What more is there for Your servant to say to You unless, with his iniquity and vileness always in mind, he humbles himself before You? Nothing among all the wonders of heaven and earth is like to You. Your works are exceedingly good, Your judgments true, and Your providence rules the whole universe. May You be praised and glorified, therefore,

O Wisdom of the Father. Let my lips and my soul and all created things unite to praise and bless You.

The Twenty-Second Chapter

REMEMBER THE INNUMERABLE GIFTS OF GOD

The Disciple

Open my heart, O Lord, to Your law and teach me to walk in the way of Your commandments. Let me understand Your will. Let me remember Your blessings—all of them and each single one of them—with great reverence and care so that henceforth I may return worthy thanks for them. I know that I am unable to give due thanks for even the least of Your gifts. I am unworthy of the benefits You have given me, and when I consider Your generosity my spirit faints away before its greatness. All that we have of soul and body, whatever we possess interiorly or exteriorly, by nature or by grace, are Your gifts and they proclaim Your goodness and mercy from which we have received all good things.

If one receives more and another less, yet all are Yours and without You nothing can be received. He who receives greater things cannot glory in his own merit or consider himself above others or behave insolently toward those who receive less. He who attributes less to himself and is the more humble and devout in returning thanks is indeed the greater and the better, while he who considers himself lower than all men and judges himself to be the least worthy, is the more fit to receive the greater blessing.

He, on the other hand, who has received fewer gifts should not be sad or impatient or envious of the richer man. Instead he should turn his mind to You and offer You the greatest praise because You give so bountifully, so freely and willingly, without regard to persons. All things come from You; therefore, You are to be praised in all things. You know what is good for each of us; and why one should receive less and another more is not for us to judge, but for You Who have marked every man's merits.

Therefore, O Lord God, I consider it a great blessing not to have many things which human judgment holds praiseworthy and glorious, for one who realizes his own poverty and vileness should not be sad or downcast at it, but rather consoled and happy because You, O God, have chosen the poor, the humble, and the despised in this world to be Your friends and servants. The truth of this is witnessed by Your Apostles, whom You made princes over all the world. Yet they lived in this world without complaining, so humble and simple, so free from malice and deceit, that they were happy even to suffer reproach for Your name and to embrace with great affection that which the world abhors.

A man who loves You and recognizes Your benefits, therefore, should be gladdened by nothing so much as by Your will, by the good pleasure of Your eternal decree. With this he should be so contented and consoled that he would wish to be the least as others wish to be the greatest; that he would be as peaceful and satisfied in the last place as in the first, and as willing to be despised, unknown and forgotten, as to be honored by others and to have more fame than they. He should prefer Your will and the love of Your honor to all else, and it should comfort him more than all the benefits which have been, or will be, given him.

The Twenty-Third Chapter

FOUR THINGS WHICH BRING GREAT PEACE

THE VOICE OF CHRIST

MY CHILD, I will teach you now the way of peace and true liberty.
- Seek, child, to do the will of others rather than your own.
- Always choose to have less rather than more.
- Look always for the last place and seek to be beneath all others.
- Always wish and pray that the will of God be fully carried out in you.
Behold, such will enter into the realm of peace and rest.

THE DISCIPLE

O Lord, this brief discourse of Yours contains much perfection. It is short in words but full of meaning and abounding in fruit. Certainly if I could only keep it faithfully, I should not be so easily disturbed. For as often as I find myself troubled and dejected, I find that I have departed from this teaching. But You Who can do all things, and Who always love what is for my soul's welfare, give me increase of grace that I may keep Your words and accomplish my salvation.

A PRAYER AGAINST BAD THOUGHTS

O Lord my God, be not far from me. O my God, hasten to help me, for varied thoughts and great fears have risen up within me, afflicting my soul. How shall I escape them unharmed? How shall I dispel them?

"I will go before you," says the Lord, "and will humble the great ones of earth. I will open the doors of the prison, and will reveal to you hidden secrets."

Do as You say, Lord, and let all evil thoughts fly from Your face. This is my hope and my only comfort—to fly to You in all tribulation, to confide in You, and to call on You from the depths of my heart and to await patiently for Your consolation.

A PRAYER FOR ENLIGHTENING THE MIND

Enlighten me, good Jesus, with the brightness of internal light, and take away all darkness from the habitation of my heart. Restrain my wandering thoughts and suppress the temptations which attack me so violently. Fight strongly for me, and vanquish these evil beasts—the alluring desires of the flesh—so that peace may come through Your power and the fullness of Your praise resound in the holy courts, which is a pure conscience. Command the winds and the tempests; say to the sea: "Be still," and to the north wind, "Do not blow," and there will be a great calm.

Send forth Your light and Your truth to shine on the earth, for I am as earth, empty and formless until You illumine me. Pour out Your grace from above. Shower my heart with heavenly dew. Open the springs of devotion to water the earth, that it may produce the best of good fruits. Lift up my heart pressed down by the weight of sins, and direct all my desires to heavenly things, that having tasted the sweetness of supernal happiness, I may find no pleasure in thinking of earthly things.

Snatch me up and deliver me from all the passing comfort of creatures, for no created thing can fully quiet and satisfy my desires. Join me to Yourself in an inseparable bond of love; because You alone can satisfy him who loves You, and without You all things are worthless.

The Twenty-Fourth Chapter

AVOIDING CURIOUS INQUIRY ABOUT THE LIVES OF OTHERS

THE VOICE OF CHRIST

MY CHILD, do not be curious. Do not trouble yourself with idle cares. What matters this or that to you? Follow Me. What is it to you if a man is such and such, if another does or says this or that? You will not have to answer for others, but you will have to give an account of yourself. Why, then, do you meddle in their affairs?

Behold, I know all men. I see everything that is done under the sun, and I know how matters stand with each—what is in his mind and what in his heart and the end to which his intention is directed. Commit all things to Me, therefore, and keep yourself in good peace. Let him who is disturbed be as restless as he will. Whatever he has said or done will fall upon himself, for he cannot deceive Me.

Do not be anxious for the shadow of a great name, for the close friendship of many, or for the particular affection of men. These things cause distraction and cast great darkness about the heart. I would willingly speak My word and reveal My secrets to you, if you would watch diligently for My coming and open your heart to Me. Be prudent, then. Watch in prayer, and in all things humble yourself.

The Twenty-Fifth Chapter

THE BASIS OF FIRM PEACE OF HEART AND TRUE PROGRESS

THE VOICE OF CHRIST

MY CHILD, I have said: "Peace I leave with you, My peace I give unto you: not as the world giveth, do I give unto you."[1]

All men desire peace but all do not care for the things that go to make true peace. My peace is with the humble and meek of heart: your peace will be in much patience. If you hear Me and follow My voice, you will be able to enjoy much peace.

---

[1] John 14:27.

THE DISCIPLE

What, then, shall I do, Lord?

THE VOICE OF CHRIST

Watch yourself in all things, in what you do and what you say. Direct your every intention toward pleasing Me alone, and desire nothing outside of Me. Do not be rash in judging the deeds and words of others, and do not entangle yourself in affairs that are not your own. Thus, it will come about that you will be disturbed little and seldom.

Yet, never to experience any disturbance or to suffer any hurt in heart or body does not belong to this present life, but rather to the state of eternal rest. Do not think, therefore, that you have found true peace if you feel no depression, or that all is well because you suffer no opposition. Do not think that all is perfect if everything happens just as you wish. And do not imagine yourself great or consider yourself especially beloved if you are filled with great devotion and sweetness. For the true lover of virtue is not known by these things, nor do the progress and perfection of a man consist in them.

THE DISCIPLE

In what do they consist, Lord?

THE VOICE OF CHRIST

They consist in offering yourself with all your heart to the divine will, not seeking what is yours either in small matters or great ones, either in temporal or eternal things, so that you will preserve equanimity and give thanks in both prosperity and adversity, seeing all things in their proper light.

If you become so brave and long-suffering in hope that you can prepare your heart to suffer still more even when all inward consolation is withdrawn, and if you do not justify yourself as though you ought not be made to suffer such great things, but acknowledge Me to be just in all My works and praise My holy name — then you will walk in the true and right path of peace, then you may have sure hope of seeing My face again in joy. If you attain to complete contempt of self, then know that you will enjoy an abundance of peace, as much as is possible in this earthly life.

The Twenty-Sixth Chapter

THE EXCELLENCE OF A FREE MIND, GAINED THROUGH PRAYER RATHER THAN BY STUDY

THE DISCIPLE

IT IS the mark of a perfect man, Lord, never to let his mind relax in attention to heavenly things, and to pass through many cares as though he had none; not as an indolent man does, but having by the certain prerogative of a free mind no disorderly affection for any created being.

Keep me, I beg You, most merciful God, from the cares of this life, lest I be too much entangled in them. Keep me from many necessities of the body, lest I be ensnared by pleasure. Keep me from all darkness of mind, lest I be broken by troubles and overcome. I do not ask deliverance from those things which worldly vanity desires so eagerly, but from those miseries which, by the common curse of humankind, oppress the soul of Your servant in punishment and keep him from entering into the liberty of spirit as often as he would.

My God, Sweetness beyond words, make bitter all the carnal comfort that draws me from love of the eternal and lures me to its evil self by the sight of some delightful good in the present. Let it not overcome me, my God. Let not flesh and blood conquer me. Let not the world and its brief glory deceive me, nor the devil trip me by his craftiness. Give me courage to resist, patience to endure, and constancy to persevere. Give me the soothing unction of Your spirit rather than all the consolations of the world, and in place of carnal love, infuse into me the love of Your name.

Behold, eating, drinking, clothing, and other necessities that sustain the body are burdensome to the fervent soul. Grant me the grace to use such comforts temperately and not to become entangled in too great a desire for them. It is not lawful to cast them aside completely, for nature must be sustained, but Your holy law forbids us to demand superfluous things and things that are simply for pleasure, else the flesh would rebel against the spirit. In these matters, I beg, let Your hand guide and direct me, so that I may not overstep the law in any way.

The Twenty-Seventh Chapter

SELF-LOVE IS THE GREATEST HINDRANCE TO THE HIGHEST GOOD

THE VOICE OF CHRIST

MY CHILD, you should give all for all, and in no way belong to yourself. You must know that self-love is more harmful to you than anything else in the world. In proportion to the love and affection you have for a thing, it will cling to you more or less. If your love is pure, simple, and well ordered, you will not be a slave to anything. Do not covet what you may not have. Do not possess anything that can hinder you or rob you of freedom.

It is strange that you do not commit yourself to Me with your whole heart, together with all that you can desire or possess. Why are you consumed with foolish sorrow? Why are you wearied with unnecessary care? Be resigned to My will and you will suffer no loss.

If you seek this or that, if you wish to be in this place or that place, to have more ease and pleasure, you will never rest or be free from care, for some defect is found in everything and everywhere someone will vex you. To obtain and multiply earthly goods, then, will not help you, but to despise them and root them out of your heart will aid. This, understand, is true not only of money and wealth, but also of ambition for honor and desire for empty praise, all of which will pass away with this world.

The place matters little if the spirit of fervor is not there; nor will peace be lasting if it is sought from the outside; if your heart has no true foundation, that is, if you are not founded in Me, you may change, but you will not better yourself. For when occasion arises and is accepted, you will find that from which you fled and worse.

A PRAYER FOR CLEANSING THE HEART AND OBTAINING HEAVENLY WISDOM

Strengthen me by the grace of Your holy spirit, O God. Give me the power to be strengthened inwardly and to empty my heart of all vain care and anxiety, so that I may not be drawn away by many desires, whether for precious things or mean ones. Let me look upon everything as passing, and upon myself as soon to pass away with them, because there is nothing lasting under the sun, where all is vanity and affliction of spirit. How wise is he who thinks thus!

Give me, Lord, heavenly wisdom to learn above all else to seek and find You, to enjoy and love You more than anything, and to consider other things as they are, as Your wisdom has ordered them. Grant me prudence to avoid the flatterer and to bear patiently with him who disagrees with me. For it is great wisdom not to be moved by the sound of words, nor to give ear to the wicked, flattering siren. Then, I shall walk safely in the way I have begun.

The Twenty-Eighth Chapter

STRENGTH AGAINST SLANDER

THE VOICE OF CHRIST

MY CHILD, do not take it to heart if some people think badly of you and say unpleasant things about you. You ought to think worse things of yourself and to believe that no one is weaker than yourself. Moreover, if you walk in the spirit you will pay little heed to fleeting words. It is no small prudence to remain silent in evil times, to turn inwardly to Me, and not to be disturbed by human opinions. Do not let your peace depend on the words of men. Their thinking well or badly of you does not make you different from what you are. Where are true peace and glory? Are they not in Me? He who neither cares to please men nor fears to displease them will enjoy great peace, for all unrest and distraction of the senses arise out of disorderly love and vain fear.

The Twenty-Ninth Chapter

HOW WE MUST CALL UPON AND BLESS THE LORD WHEN TROUBLE PRESSES

THE DISCIPLE

BLESSED BE Your name forever, O Lord, Who have willed that this temptation and trouble come upon me. I cannot escape it, yet I must fly to You that You may help me and turn it to my good. Now I am troubled, Lord, and my heart is not at rest, for I am greatly afflicted by this present suffering.

Beloved Father, what shall I say? I am straitened in harsh ways. Save me from this hour to which, however, I am come that You may be glorified when I am deeply humbled and freed by You. May it please You, then, to deliver me, Lord, for what can I, poor wretch that I am, do or where can I go without You? Give me patience, Lord, even now. Help me, my God, and I will not be afraid however much I may be distressed.

But here, in the midst of these troubles, what shall I say? Your will be done, Lord. I have richly deserved to be troubled and distressed. But I must bear it. Would that I could do so patiently, until the storm passes and calm returns! Yet Your almighty hand can take this temptation from me, or lighten its attack so that I do not altogether sink beneath it, as You, my God, my Mercy, have very often done for me before. And the more difficult my plight, the easier for You is this change of the right hand of the Most High.

The Thirtieth Chapter

THE QUEST OF DIVINE HELP AND CONFIDENCE IN REGAINING GRACE

THE VOICE OF CHRIST

MY CHILD, I am the Lord Who gives strength in the day of trouble. Come to Me when all is not well with you. Your tardiness in turning to prayer is the greatest obstacle to heavenly consolation, for before you pray earnestly to Me you first seek many comforts and take pleasure in outward things. Thus, all things are of little profit to you until you realize that I am the one Who saves those who trust in Me, and that outside of Me there is no worth-while help, or any useful counsel or lasting remedy.

But now, after the tempest, take courage, grow strong once more in the light of My mercies; for I am near, says the Lord, to restore all things not only to the full but with abundance and above measure. Is anything difficult for Me? Or shall I be as one who promises and does not act? Where is your faith? Stand firm and persevere. Be a man of endurance and courage, and consolation will come to you in due time. Wait for Me; wait—and I will come to heal you.

It is only a temptation that troubles you, a vain fear that terrifies you.

Of what use is anxiety about the future? Does it bring you anything but trouble upon trouble? Sufficient for the day is the evil thereof. It is foolish and useless to be either grieved or happy about future things which perhaps may never happen. But it is human to be deluded by such imaginations, and the sign of a weak soul to be led on by suggestions of the enemy. For he does not care whether he overcomes you by love of the present or fear of the future.

Let not your heart be troubled, therefore, nor let it be afraid. Believe in Me and trust in My mercy. When you think you are far from Me, then often I am very near you. When you judge that almost all is lost, then very often you are in the way of gaining great merit.

All is not lost when things go contrary to your wishes. You ought not judge according to present feelings, nor give in to any trouble whenever it comes, or take it as though all hope of escape were lost. And do not consider yourself forsaken if I send some temporary hardship, or withdraw the consolation you desire. For this is the way to the kingdom of heaven, and without doubt it is better for you and the rest of My servants to be tried in adversities than to have all things as you wish. I know your secret thoughts, and I know that it is profitable for your salvation to be left sometimes in despondency lest perhaps you be puffed up by success and fancy yourself to be what you are not.

What I have given, I can take away and restore when it pleases Me. What I give remains Mine, and thus when I take it away I take nothing that is yours, for every good gift and every perfect gift is Mine.

If I send you trouble and adversity, do not fret or let your heart be downcast. I can raise you quickly up again and turn all your sorrow into joy. I am no less just and worthy of great praise when I deal with you in this way.

If you think aright and view things in their true light, you should never be so dejected and saddened by adversity, but rather rejoice and give thanks, considering it a matter of special joy that I afflict you with sorrow and do not spare you. "As the Father hath loved Me, so also I love you," I said to My disciples, and I certainly did not send them out to temporal joys but rather to great struggles, not to honors but to contempt, not to idleness, but to labors, not to rest but to bring forth much fruit in patience. Do you, My child, remember these words.

The Thirty-First Chapter

TO FIND THE CREATOR, FORSAKE ALL CREATURES

The Disciple

O Lord, I am in sore need still of greater grace if I am to arrive at the point where no man and no created thing can be an obstacle to me. For as long as anything holds me back, I cannot freely fly to You. He that said "Oh that I had wings like a dove, that I might fly away and be at rest!"[1] desired to fly freely to You. Who is more at rest than he who aims at nothing but God? And who more free than the man who desires nothing on earth?

It is well, then, to pass over all creation, perfectly to abandon self, and to see in ecstasy of mind that You, the Creator of all, have no likeness among all Your creatures, and that unless a man be freed from all creatures, he cannot attend freely to the Divine. The reason why so few contemplative persons are found, is that so few know how to separate themselves entirely from what is transitory and created.

For this, indeed, great grace is needed, grace that will raise the soul and lift it up above itself. Unless a man be elevated in spirit, free from all creatures, and completely united to God, all his knowledge and possessions are of little moment. He who considers anything great except the one, immense, eternal good will long be little and lie groveling on the earth. Whatever is not God is nothing and must be accounted as nothing.

There is great difference between the wisdom of an enlightened and devout man and the learning of a well-read and brilliant scholar, for the knowledge which flows down from divine sources is much nobler than that laboriously acquired by human industry.

Many there are who desire contemplation, but who do not care to do the things which contemplation requires. It is also a great obstacle to be satisfied with externals and sensible things, and to have so little of perfect mortification. I know not what it is, or by what spirit we are led, or to what we pretend—we who wish to be called spiritual—that we spend so much labor and even more anxiety on things that are transitory and mean, while we seldom or never advert with full consciousness to our interior concerns.

Alas, after very little recollection we falter, not weighing our deeds by strict examination. We pay no attention to where our affections lie, nor do we deplore the fact that our actions are impure.

Remember that because all flesh had corrupted its course, the great deluge followed. Since, then, our interior affection is corrupt, it must be that the action which follows from it, the index as it were of our lack of inward strength, is also corrupt. Out of a pure heart come the fruits of a good life.

People are wont to ask how much a man has done, but they think little of the virtue with which he acts. They ask: Is he strong? rich? handsome? a good writer? a good singer? or a good worker? They say little,

---

[1] Ps. 54:7.

however, about how poor he is in spirit, how patient and meek, how devout and spiritual. Nature looks to his outward appearance; grace turns to his inward being. The one often errs, the other trusts in God and is not deceived.

The Thirty-Second Chapter

SELF-DENIAL AND THE RENUNCIATION OF EVIL APPETITES

THE VOICE OF CHRIST

MY CHILD, you can never be perfectly free unless you completely renounce self, for all who seek their own interest and who love themselves are bound in fetters. They are unsettled by covetousness and curiosity, always searching for ease and not for the things of Christ, often devising and framing that which will not last, for anything that is not of God will fail completely.

Hold to this short and perfect advice, therefore: *give up your desires and you will find rest.* Think upon it in your heart, and when you have put it into practice you will understand all things.

THE DISCIPLE

But this, Lord, is not the work of one day, nor is it mere child's play; indeed, in this brief sentence is included all the perfection of holy persons.

THE VOICE OF CHRIST

My child, you should not turn away or be downcast when you hear the way of the perfect. Rather you ought to be spurred on the more toward their sublime heights, or at least be moved to seek perfection. I would this were the case with you—that you had progressed to the point where you no longer loved self but simply awaited My bidding and his whom I have placed as father over you. Then you would please Me very much, and your whole life would pass in peace and joy. But you have yet many things which you must give up, and unless you resign them entirely to Me you will not obtain that which you ask.

"I counsel thee to buy of me gold, fire-tried, that thou mayest be made rich"[1] — rich in heavenly wisdom which treads underfoot all that is low. Put aside earthly wisdom, all human self-complacency.

I have said: exchange what is precious and valued among men for that which is considered contemptible. For true heavenly wisdom — not to think highly of self and not to seek glory on earth — does indeed seem mean and small and is well-nigh forgotten, as many men praise it with their mouths but shy far away from it in their lives. Yet this heavenly wisdom is a pearl of great price, which is hidden from many.

The Thirty-Third Chapter

RESTLESSNESS OF SOUL — DIRECTING OUR FINAL INTENTION TOWARD GOD

The Voice of Christ

My CHILD, do not trust in your present feeling, for it will soon give way to another. As long as you live you will be subject to changeableness in spite of yourself. You will become merry at one time and sad at another, now peaceful but again disturbed, at one moment devout and the next indevout, sometimes diligent while at other times lazy, now grave and again flippant.

But the man who is wise and whose spirit is well instructed stands superior to these changes. He pays no attention to what he feels in himself or from what quarter the wind of fickleness blows, so long as the whole intention of his mind is conducive to his proper and desired end. For thus he can stand undivided, unchanged, and unshaken, with the singleness of his intention directed unwaveringly toward Me, even in the midst of so many changing events. And the purer this singleness of intention is, with so much the more constancy does he pass through many storms.

But in many ways the eye of pure intention grows dim, because it is attracted to any delightful thing that it meets. Indeed, it is rare to find one who is entirely free from all taint of self-seeking. The Jews of old, for example, came to Bethany to Martha and Mary, not for Jesus' sake alone, but in order to see Lazarus.

---

[1] Apoc. 3:18.

The eye of your intention, therefore, must be cleansed so that it is single and right. It must be directed toward Me, despite all the objects which may interfere.

The Thirty-Fourth Chapter

GOD IS SWEET ABOVE ALL THINGS AND IN ALL THINGS TO THOSE WHO LOVE HIM

THE DISCIPLE

BEHOLD, MY God and my all! What more do I wish for; what greater happiness can I desire? O sweet and delicious word! But sweet only to him who loves it, and not to the world or the things that are in the world.

My God and my all! These words are enough for him who understands, and for him who loves it is a joy to repeat them often. For when You are present, all things are delightful; when You are absent, all things become loathsome. It is You Who give a heart tranquillity, great peace and festive joy. It is You Who make us think well of all things, and praise You in all things. Without You nothing can give pleasure for very long, for if it is to be pleasing and tasteful, Your grace and the seasoning of Your wisdom must be in it. What is there that can displease him whose happiness is in You? And, on the contrary, what can satisfy him whose delight is not in You?

The wise men of the world, the men who lust for the flesh, are wanting in Your wisdom, because in the world is found the utmost vanity, and in the flesh is death. But they who follow You by disdaining worldly things and mortifying the flesh are known to be truly wise, for they are transported from vanity to truth, from flesh to spirit. By such as these God is relished, and whatever good is found in creatures they turn to praise of the Creator. But great—yes, very great, indeed—is the difference between delight in the Creator and in the creature, in eternity and in time, in Light uncreated and in the light that is reflected.

O Light eternal, surpassing all created brightness, flash forth the lightning from above and enlighten the inmost recesses of my heart. Cleanse, cheer, enlighten, and vivify my spirit with all its powers, that it may cleave to You in ecstasies of joy. Oh, when will that happy and wished-for hour come, that You may fill me with Your presence and become all in all to me? So long as this is not given me, my joy will not be complete.

The old man, alas, yet lives within me. He has not yet been entirely crucified; he is not yet entirely dead. He still lusts strongly against the spirit, and he will not leave the kingdom of my soul in peace. But You, Who can command the power of the sea and calm the tumult of its waves, arise and help me. Scatter the nations that delight in war; crush them in Your sight. Show forth I beg, Your wonderful works and let Your right hand be glorified, because for me there is no other hope or refuge except in You, O Lord, my God.

The Thirty-Fifth Chapter

THERE IS NO SECURITY FROM TEMPTATION IN THIS LIFE

THE VOICE OF CHRIST

MY CHILD, in this life you are never safe, and as long as you live the weapons of the spirit will ever be necessary to you. You dwell among enemies. You are subject to attack from the right and the left. If, therefore, you do not guard yourself from every quarter with the shield of patience, you will not remain long unscathed.

Moreover, if you do not steadily set your heart on Me, with a firm will to suffer everything for My sake, you will not be able to bear the heat of this battle or to win the crown of the blessed. You ought, therefore, to pass through all these things manfully and to oppose a strong hand to whatever stands in your way. For to him who triumphs heavenly bread is given, while for him who is too lazy to fight there remains much misery.

If you look for rest in this life, how will you attain to everlasting rest? Dispose yourself, then, not for much rest but for great patience. Seek true peace, not on earth but in heaven; not in men or in other creatures but in God alone. For love of God you should undergo all things cheerfully, all labors and sorrows, temptations and trials, anxieties, weaknesses, necessities, injuries, slanders, rebukes, humiliations, confusions, corrections, and contempt. For these are helps to virtue. These are the trials of Christ's recruit. These form the heavenly crown. For a little brief labor I will give an everlasting crown, and for passing confusion, glory that is eternal.

Do you think that you will always have spiritual consolations as you desire? My saints did not always have them. Instead, they had many afflictions, temptations of various kinds, and great desolation. Yet they bore them all patiently. They placed their confidence in God rather than in themselves, knowing that the sufferings of this life are not worthy to be compared with the glory that is to come. And you—do you wish to have at once that which others have scarcely obtained after many tears and great labors?

Wait for the Lord, act manfully, and have courage. Do not lose trust. Do not turn back but devote your body and soul constantly to God's glory. I will reward you most plentifully. I will be with you in every tribulation.

The Thirty-Sixth Chapter

THE VAIN JUDGMENTS OF MEN

THE VOICE OF CHRIST

MY CHILD, trust firmly in the Lord, and do not fear the judgment of men when conscience tells you that you are upright and innocent. For it is good and blessed to suffer such things, and they will not weigh heavily on the humble heart that trusts in God rather than in itself. Many men say many things, and therefore little faith is to be put in them.

Likewise, it is impossible to satisfy all men. Although Paul tried to please all in the Lord, and became all things to all men, yet he made little of their opinions. He labored abundantly for the edification and salvation of others, as much as lay in him and as much as he could, but he could not escape being sometimes judged and despised by others. Therefore, he committed all to God Who knows all things, and defended himself by his patience and humility against the tongues of those who spoke unjustly or thought foolish things and lies, or made accusations against him. Sometimes, indeed, he did answer them, but only lest his silence scandalize the weak.

Who are you, then, that you should be afraid of mortal man? Today he is here, tomorrow he is not seen. Fear God and you will not be afraid of the terrors of men. What can anyone do to you by word or injury? He hurts himself rather than you, and no matter who he may be he cannot escape the judgment of God. Keep God before your eyes, therefore, and do not quarrel with peevish words.

If it seems, then, that you are worsted and that you suffer undeserved shame, do not repine over it and do not lessen your crown by impatience. Look instead to heaven, to Me, Who have power to deliver you from all disgrace and injury, and to render to everyone according to his works.

The Thirty-Seventh Chapter

PURE AND ENTIRE RESIGNATION OF SELF TO OBTAIN FREEDOM OF HEART

THE VOICE OF CHRIST

MY CHILD, renounce self and you shall find Me. Give up your own self-will, your possessions, and you shall always gain. For once you resign yourself irrevocably, greater grace will be given you.

THE DISCIPLE

How often, Lord, shall I resign myself? And in what shall I forsake myself?

THE VOICE OF CHRIST

Always, at every hour, in small matters as well as great—I except nothing. In all things I wish you to be stripped of self. How otherwise can you be mine or I yours unless you be despoiled of your own will both inwardly and outwardly? The sooner you do this the better it will be for you, and the more fully and sincerely you do it the more you will please Me and the greater gain you will merit.

Some there are who resign themselves, but with certain reservation; they do not trust fully in God and therefore they try to provide for themselves. Others, again, at first offer all, but afterward are assailed by temptation and return to what they have renounced, thereby making no progress in virtue. These will not reach the true liberty of a pure heart nor the grace of happy friendship with Me unless they first make a full resignation and a daily sacrifice of themselves. Without this no fruitful union lasts nor will last.

I have said to you very often, and now I say again: forsake yourself, renounce yourself and you shall enjoy great inward peace. Give all for all. Ask nothing, demand nothing in return. Trust purely and without hesitation in Me, and you shall possess Me. You will be free of heart and darkness will not overwhelm you.

Strive for this, pray for this, desire this—to be stripped of all selfishness and naked to follow the naked Jesus, to die to self and live forever for Me. Then all vain imaginations, all wicked disturbances and superfluous cares will vanish. Then also immoderate fear will leave you and inordinate love will die.

The Thirty-Eighth Chapter

THE RIGHT ORDERING OF EXTERNAL AFFAIRS; RECOURSE TO GOD IN DANGERS

THE VOICE OF CHRIST

MY CHILD, you must strive diligently to be inwardly free, to have mastery over yourself everywhere, in every external act and occupation, that all things be subject to you and not you to them, that you be the master and director of your actions, not a slave or a mere hired servant. You should be rather a free man and a true Hebrew, arising to the status and freedom of the children of God who stand above present things to contemplate those which are eternal; who look upon passing affairs with the left eye and upon those of heaven with the right; whom temporal things do not so attract that they cling to them, but who rather put these things to such proper service as is ordained and instituted by God, the great Workmaster, Who leaves nothing unordered in His creation.

If, likewise, in every happening you are not content simply with outward appearances, if you do not regard with carnal eyes things which you see and hear, but whatever be the affair, enter with Moses into the tabernacle to ask advice of the Lord, you will sometimes hear the divine answer and return instructed in many things present and to come. For Moses always had recourse to the tabernacle for the solution of doubts and questions, and fled to prayer for support in dangers and the evil deeds of men. So you also should take refuge in the secret chamber of your heart, begging earnestly for divine aid.

For this reason, as we read, Joshua and the children of Israel were deceived by the Gibeonites because they did not first seek counsel of the Lord, but trusted too much in fair words and hence were deceived by false piety.

The Thirty-Ninth Chapter

A MAN SHOULD NOT BE UNDULY SOLICITOUS ABOUT HIS AFFAIRS

THE VOICE OF CHRIST

MY CHILD, always commit your cause to Me. I will dispose of it rightly in good time. Await My ordering of it and it will be to your advantage.

THE DISCIPLE

Lord, I willingly commit all things to You, for my anxiety can profit me little. But I would that I were not so concerned about the future, and instead offered myself without hesitation to Your good pleasure.

THE VOICE OF CHRIST

My child, it often happens that a man seeks ardently after something he desires and then when he has attained it he begins to think that it is not at all desirable; for affections do not remain fixed on the same thing, but rather flit from one to another. It is no very small matter, therefore, for a man to forsake himself even in things that are very small.

A man's true progress consists in denying himself, and the man who has denied himself is truly free and secure. The old enemy, however, setting himself against all good, never ceases to tempt them, but day and night plots dangerous snares to cast the unwary into the net of deceit. "Watch ye and pray," says the Lord, "that ye enter not into temptation."[1]

---

[1] Matt. 16:41.

The Fortieth Chapter

MAN HAS NO GOOD IN HIMSELF AND CAN GLORY IN NOTHING

THE DISCIPLE

LORD, WHAT is man that You are mindful of him, or the son of man that You visit him? What has man deserved that You should give him Your grace? What cause have I, Lord, to complain if You desert me, or what objection can I have if You do not do what I ask? This I may think and say in all truth: "Lord, I am nothing, of myself I have nothing that is good; I am lacking in all things, and I am ever tending toward nothing. And unless I have Your help and am inwardly strengthened by You, I become quite lukewarm and lax."

But You, Lord, are always the same. You remain forever, always good, just, and holy; doing all things rightly, justly, and holily, disposing them wisely. I, however, who am more ready to go backward than forward, do not remain always in one state, for I change with the seasons. Yet my condition quickly improves when it pleases You and when You reach forth Your helping hand. For You alone, without human aid, can help me and strengthen me so greatly that my heart shall no more change but be converted and rest solely in You. Hence, if I knew well how to cast aside all earthly consolation, either to attain devotion or because of the necessity which, in the absence of human solace, compels me to seek You alone, then I could deservedly hope for Your grace and rejoice in the gift of new consolation.

Thanks be to You from Whom all things come, whenever it is well with me. In Your sight I am vanity and nothingness, a weak, unstable man. In what, therefore, can I glory, and how can I wish to be highly regarded? Is it because I am nothing? This, too, is utterly vain. Indeed, the greatest vanity is the evil plague of empty self-glory, because it draws one away from true glory and robs one of heavenly grace. For when a man is pleased with himself he displeases You, when he pants after human praise he is deprived of true virtue. But it is true glory and holy exultation to glory in You and not in self, to rejoice in Your name rather than in one's own virtue, and not to delight in any creature except for Your sake.

Let Your name, not mine, be praised. Let Your work, not mine, be magnified. Let Your holy name be blessed, but let no human praise be given to me. You are my glory. You are the joy of my heart. In You I will glory and rejoice all the day, and for myself I will glory in nothing but my infirmities.

Let the Jews seek the glory that comes from another. I will seek that which comes from God alone. All human glory, all temporal honor, all worldly position is truly vanity and foolishness compared to Your ever-lasting glory. O my Truth, my Mercy, my God, O Blessed Trinity, to You alone be praise and honor, power and glory, throughout all the endless ages of ages.

The Forty-First Chapter

CONTEMPT FOR ALL EARTHLY HONOR

THE VOICE OF CHRIST

MY CHILD, do not take it to heart if you see others honored and advanced, while you yourself are despised and humbled. Lift up your heart to Me in heaven and the contempt of men on earth will not grieve you.

THE DISCIPLE

Lord, we are blinded and quickly misled by vanity. If I examine myself rightly, no injury has ever been done me by any creature; hence I have nothing for which to make just complaint to You. But I have sinned often and gravely against You; therefore is every creature in arms against me. Confusion and contempt should in justice come upon me, but to You due praise, honor, and glory. And unless I prepare myself to be willingly despised and forsaken by every creature, to be considered absolutely nothing, I cannot have interior peace and strength, nor can I be enlightened spiritually or completely united with You.

The Forty-Second Chapter

PEACE IS NOT TO BE PLACED IN MEN

THE VOICE OF CHRIST

MY CHILD, if you place your peace in any creature because of your own feeling or for the sake of his company, you will be unsettled and entangled. But if you have recourse to the everliving and abiding Truth, you will not grieve if a friend should die or forsake you. Your love for your friend should be grounded in Me, and for My sake you should love whoever seems to be good and is very dear to you in this life. Without Me friendship has no strength and cannot endure. Love which I do not bind is neither true nor pure.

You ought, therefore, to be so dead to such human affections as to wish as far as lies within you to be without the fellowship of men. Man draws nearer to God in proportion as he withdraws farther from all earthly comfort. And he ascends higher to God as he descends lower into himself and grows more vile in his own eyes. He who attributes any good to himself hinders God's grace from coming into his heart, for the grace of the Holy Spirit seeks always the humble heart.

If you knew how to annihilate yourself completely and empty yourself of all created love, then I should overflow in you with great grace. When you look to creatures, the sight of the Creator is taken from you. Learn, therefore, to conquer yourself in all things for the sake of your Maker. Then will you be able to attain to divine knowledge. But anything, no matter how small, that is loved and regarded inordinately keeps you back from the highest good and corrupts the soul.

The Forty-Third Chapter

BEWARE VAIN AND WORLDLY KNOWLEDGE

THE VOICE OF CHRIST

MY CHILD, do not let the fine-sounding and subtle words of men deceive you. For the kingdom of heaven consists not in talk but in virtue. Attend, rather, to My words which enkindle the heart and enlighten the mind, which excite contrition and abound in manifold consolations. Never read them for the purpose of appearing more learned or more wise. Apply yourself to mortifying your vices, for this will benefit you more than your understanding of many difficult questions.

Though you shall have read and learned many things, it will always be necessary for you to return to this one principle: I am He who teaches man knowledge, and to the little ones I give a clearer understanding than can be taught by man. He to whom I speak will soon be wise and his soul will profit. But woe to those who inquire of men about many curious things, and care very little about the way they serve Me.

The time will come when Christ, the Teacher of teachers, the Lord of angels, will appear to hear the lessons of all—that is, to examine the conscience of everyone. Then He will search Jerusalem with lamps and the hidden things of darkness will be brought to light and the arguings of men's tongues be silenced.

I am He Who in one moment so enlightens the humble mind that it comprehends more of eternal truth than could be learned by ten years in the schools. I teach without noise of words or clash of opinions, without ambition for honor or confusion of argument.

I am He Who teaches man to despise earthly possessions and to loathe present things, to ask after the eternal, to hunger for heaven, to fly honors and to bear with scandals, to place all hope in Me, to desire nothing apart from Me, and to love Me ardently above all things. For a certain man by loving Me intimately learned divine truths and spoke wonders. He profited more by leaving all things than by studying subtle questions.

To some I speak of common things, to others of special matters. To some I appear with sweetness in signs and figures, and to others I appear in great light and reveal mysteries. The voice of books is but a single voice, yet it does not teach all men alike, because I within them am the Teacher and the Truth, the Examiner of hearts, the Understander of thoughts, the Promoter of acts, distributing to each as I see fit.

The Forty-Fourth Chapter

DO NOT BE CONCERNED ABOUT OUTWARD THINGS

THE VOICE OF CHRIST

MY CHILD, there are many matters of which it is well for you to be ignorant, and to consider yourself as one who is dead upon the earth and to whom the whole world is crucified. There are many things, too, which it is well to pass by with a deaf ear, thinking, instead, of what is more to your peace. It is more profitable to turn away from things which displease you and to leave to every man his own opinion than to take part in quarrelsome talk. If you stand well with God and look to His judgment, you will more easily bear being worsted.

THE DISCIPLE

To what have we come, Lord? Behold, we bewail a temporal loss. We labor and fret for a small gain, while loss of the soul is forgotten and scarcely ever returns to mind. That which is of little or no value claims our attention, whereas that which is of highest necessity is neglected—all because man gives himself wholly to outward things. And unless he withdraws himself quickly, he willingly lies immersed in externals.

The Forty-Fifth Chapter

ALL MEN ARE NOT TO BE BELIEVED, FOR IT IS EASY TO ERR IN SPEECH

THE DISCIPLE

GRANT ME help in my needs, O Lord, for the aid of man is useless. How often have I failed to find faithfulness in places where I thought I possessed it! And how many times I have found it where I least expected it! Vain, therefore, is hope in men, but the salvation of the just is in You, O God. Blessed be Your name, O Lord my God, in everything that befalls us.

We are weak and unstable, quickly deceived and changed. Who is the man that is able to guard himself with such caution and care as not sometimes to fall into deception or perplexity? He who confides in You, O Lord, and seeks You with a simple heart does not fall so easily. And if some trouble should come upon him, no matter how entangled in it he may be, he will be more quickly delivered and comforted by You. For You will not forsake him who trusts in You to the very end.

Rare is the friend who remains faithful through all his friend's distress. But You, Lord, and You alone, are entirely faithful in all things; other than You, there is none so faithful.

Oh, how wise is that holy soul[1] who said: "My mind is firmly settled and founded in Christ." If that were true of me, human fear would not so easily cause me anxiety, nor would the darts of words disturb. But who can foresee all things and provide against all evils? And if things foreseen have often hurt, can those which are unlooked for do otherwise than wound us gravely? Why, indeed, have I not provided better for my wretched self? Why, too, have I so easily kept faith in others? We

---

[1] St. Agatha.

are but men, however, nothing more than weak men, although we are thought by many to be, and are called, angels.

In whom shall I put my faith, Lord? In whom but You? You are the truth which does not deceive and cannot be deceived. Every man, on the other hand, is a liar, weak, unstable, and likely to err, especially in words, so that one ought not to be too quick to believe even that which seems, on the face of it, to sound true. How wise was Your warning to beware of men; that a man's enemies are those of his own household; that we should not believe if anyone says: "Behold he is here, or behold he is there."

I have been taught to my own cost, and I hope it has given me greater caution, not greater folly. "Beware," they say, "beware and keep to yourself what I tell you!" Then while I keep silent, believing that the matter is secret, he who asks me to be silent cannot remain silent himself, but immediately betrays both me and himself, and goes his way. From tales of this kind and from such careless men protect me, O Lord, lest I fall into their hands and into their ways. Put in my mouth words that are true and steadfast and keep far from me the crafty tongue, because what I am not willing to suffer I ought by all means to shun.

Oh, how good and how peaceful it is to be silent about others, not to believe without discrimination all that is said, not easily to report it further, to reveal oneself to few, always to seek You as the discerner of hearts, and not to be blown away by every wind of words, but to wish that all things, within and beyond us, be done according to the pleasure of Thy will.

How conducive it is for the keeping of heavenly grace to fly the gaze of men, not to seek abroad things which seem to cause admiration, but to follow with utmost diligence those which give fervor and amendment of life! How many have been harmed by having their virtue known and praised too hastily! And how truly profitable it has been when grace remained hidden during this frail life, which is all temptation and warfare!

The Forty-Sixth Chapter

TRUST IN GOD AGAINST SLANDER

THE VOICE OF CHRIST

MY CHILD, stand firm and trust in Me. For what are words but words? They fly through the air but hurt not a stone. If you are guilty, consider how you would gladly amend. If you are not conscious of any fault, think that you wish to bear this for the sake of God. It is little enough for you occasionally to endure words, since you are not yet strong enough to bear hard blows.

And why do such small matters pierce you to the heart, unless because you are still carnal and pay more heed to men than you ought? You do not wish to be reproved for your faults and you seek shelter in excuses because you are afraid of being despised. But look into yourself more thoroughly and you will learn that the world is still alive in you, in a vain desire to please men. For when you shrink from being abased and confounded for your failings, it is plain indeed that you are not truly humble or truly dead to the world, and that the world is not crucified in you.

Harken to My word, and you will not value ten thousand words of men. Behold, if every malicious thing that could possibly be invented were uttered against you, what harm could it do if you ignored it all and gave it no more thought than you would a blade of grass? Could it so much as pluck one hair from your head?

He who does not keep his heart within him, and who does not have God before his eyes is easily moved by a word of disparagement. He who trusts in Me, on the other hand, and who has no desire to stand by his own judgment, will be free from the fear of men. For I am the judge and discerner of all secrets. I know how all things happen. I know who causes injury and who suffers it. From Me that word proceeded, and with My permission it happened, that out of many hearts thoughts may be revealed. I shall judge the guilty and the innocent; but I have wished beforehand to try them both by secret judgment.

The testimony of man is often deceiving, but My judgment is true — it will stand and not be overthrown. It is hidden from many and made known to but a few. Yet it is never mistaken and cannot be mistaken even though it does not seem right in the eyes of the unwise.

To Me, therefore, you ought to come in every decision, not depending on your own judgment. For the just man will not be disturbed, no matter what may befall him from God. Even if an unjust charge be made against him he will not be much troubled. Neither will he exult vainly if through others he is justly acquitted. He considers that it is I Who search the hearts and inmost thoughts of men, that I do not judge according to the face of things or human appearances. For what the judgment of men considers praiseworthy is often worthy of blame in My sight.

THE DISCIPLE

O Lord God, just Judge, strong and patient, You Who know the weakness and depravity of men, be my strength and all my confidence, for my own conscience is not sufficient for me. You know what I do not know, and, therefore, I ought to humble myself whenever I am accused and bear it meekly. Forgive me, then, in Your mercy for my every failure in this regard, and give me once more the grace of greater endurance. Better to me is Your abundant mercy in obtaining pardon than the justice which I imagine in defending the secrets of my conscience. And though I am not conscious to myself of any fault, yet I cannot thereby justify myself, because without Your mercy no man living will be justified in Your sight.

The Forty-Seventh Chapter

EVERY TRIAL MUST BE BORNE FOR THE SAKE OF ETERNAL LIFE

THE VOICE OF CHRIST

MY CHILD, do not let the labors which you have taken up for My sake break you, and do not let troubles, from whatever source, cast you down; but in everything let My promise strengthen and console you. I am able to reward you beyond all means and measure.

You will not labor here long, nor will you always be oppressed by sorrows. Wait a little while and you will see a speedy end of evils. The hour will come when all labor and trouble shall be no more. All that passes away with time is trivial.

What you do, do well. Work faithfully in My vineyard. I will be your reward. Write, read, sing, mourn, keep silence, pray, and bear hardships like a man. Eternal life is worth all these and greater battles. Peace will come on a day which is known to the Lord, and then there shall be no day or night as at present but perpetual light, infinite brightness, lasting peace, and safe repose. Then you will not say: "Who shall deliver me from the body of this death?" nor will you cry: "Woe is me, because my sojourn is prolonged." For then death will be banished, and there will be health unfailing. There will be no anxiety then, but blessed joy and sweet, noble companionship.

If you could see the everlasting crowns of the saints in heaven, and the great glory wherein they now rejoice—they who were once considered contemptible in this world and, as it were, unworthy of life itself—you would certainly humble yourself at once to the very earth, and seek to be subject to all rather than to command even one. Nor would you desire the pleasant days of this life, but rather be glad to suffer for God, considering it your greatest gain to be counted as nothing among men.

Oh, if these things appealed to you and penetrated deeply into your heart, how could you dare to complain even once? Ought not all trials be borne for the sake of everlasting life? In truth, the loss or gain of God's kingdom is no small matter.

Lift up your countenance to heaven, then. Behold Me, and with Me all My saints. They had great trials in this life, but now they rejoice. They are consoled. Now they are safe and at rest. And they shall abide with Me for all eternity in the kingdom of My Father.

The Forty-Eighth Chapter

THE DAY OF ETERNITY AND THE DISTRESSES OF THIS LIFE

THE DISCIPLE

O MOST happy mansion of the city above! O most bright day of eternity, which night does not darken, but which the highest truth ever enlightens! O day, ever joyful and ever secure, which never changes its state to the opposite! Oh, that this day shine forth, that all these temporal things come to an end! It envelops the saints all resplendent with heavenly brightness, but it appears far off as through a glass to us wanderers on the earth. The citizens of heaven know how joyful that day is, but the exiled sons of Eve mourn that this one is bitter and tedious.

The days of this life are short and evil, full of grief and distress. Here man is defiled by many sins, ensnared in many passions, enslaved by many fears, and burdened with many cares. He is distracted by many curiosities and entangled in many vanities, surrounded by many errors and worn by many labors, oppressed by temptations, weakened by pleasures, and tortured by want.

Oh, when will these evils end? When shall I be freed from the miserable slavery of vice? When, Lord, shall I think of You alone? When shall I fully rejoice in You? When shall I be without hindrance, in true liberty, free from every grievance of mind and body? When will there be solid peace, undisturbed and secure, inward peace and outward peace, peace secured on every side? O good Jesus, when shall I stand to gaze upon You? When shall I contemplate the glory of Your kingdom? When will You be all in all to me? Oh, when shall I be with You in that kingdom of Yours, which You have prepared for Your beloved from all eternity?

I am left poor and exiled in a hostile land, where every day sees wars and very great misfortunes. Console my banishment, assuage my sorrow. My whole desire is for You. Whatever solace this world offers is a burden to me. I desire to enjoy You intimately, but I cannot attain to it. I wish to cling fast to heavenly things, but temporal affairs and unmortified passions bear me down. I wish in mind to be above all things, but I am forced by the flesh to be unwillingly subject to them. Thus, I fight with myself, unhappy that I am, and am become a burden to myself, while my spirit seeks to rise upward and my flesh to sink downward. Oh, what inward suffering I undergo when I consider heavenly things; when I pray, a multitude of carnal thoughts rush upon me!

O my God, do not remove Yourself far from me, and depart not in anger from Your servant. Dart forth Your lightning and disperse them; send forth Your arrows and let the phantoms of the enemy be put to flight. Draw my senses toward You and make me forget all worldly things. Grant me the grace to cast away quickly all vicious imaginings and to scorn them. Aid me, O heavenly Truth, that no vanity may move me. Come, heavenly Sweetness, and let all impurity fly from before Your face.

Pardon me also, and deal mercifully with me, as often as I think of anything besides You in prayer. For I confess truly that I am accustomed to be very much distracted. Very often I am not where bodily I stand or sit; rather, I am where my thoughts carry me. Where my thoughts are, there am I; and frequently my thoughts are where my love is. That which naturally delights, or is by habit pleasing, comes to me quickly. Hence You Who are Truth itself, have plainly said: "For where your treasure is, there is your heart also." If I love heaven, I think willingly of heavenly things. If I love the world, I rejoice at the happiness of the world and grieve at its troubles. If I love the flesh, I often imagine things that are carnal. If I love the spirit, I delight in thinking of spiritual matters. For whatever I love, I am willing to speak and hear about.

Blessed is the man who for Your sake, O Lord, dismisses all creatures, does violence to nature, crucifies the desires of the flesh in fervor of spirit, so that with serene conscience he can offer You a pure prayer and, having excluded all earthly things inwardly and outwardly, becomes worthy to enter into the heavenly choirs.

The Forty-Ninth Chapter

THE DESIRE OF ETERNAL LIFE; THE GREAT REWARDS PROMISED TO THOSE WHO STRUGGLE

The Voice of Christ

MY CHILD, when you feel the desire for everlasting happiness poured out upon you from above, and when you long to depart out of the tabernacle of the body that you may contemplate My glory without threat of change, open wide your heart and receive this holy inspiration with all eagerness. Give deepest thanks to the heavenly Goodness which deals with you so understandingly, visits you so mercifully, stirs you so fervently, and sustains you so powerfully lest under your own weight you sink down to earthly things. For you obtain this not by your own thought or effort, but simply by the condescension of heavenly grace and divine regard. And the purpose of it is that you may advance in virtue and in greater humility, that you may prepare yourself for future trials, that you may strive to cling to Me with all the affection of your heart, and may serve Me with a fervent will.

My child, often, when the fire is burning the flame does not ascend without smoke. Likewise, the desires of some burn toward heavenly things, and yet they are not free from temptations of carnal affection. Therefore, it is not altogether for the pure honor of God that they act when they petition Him so earnestly. Such, too, is often your desire which you profess to be so strong. For that which is alloyed with self-interest is not pure and perfect.

Ask, therefore, not for what is pleasing and convenient to yourself, but for what is acceptable to Me and is for My honor, because if you judge rightly, you ought to prefer and follow My will, not your own desire or whatever things you wish.

I know your longings and I have heard your frequent sighs. Already you wish to be in the liberty of the glory of the sons of God. Already you desire the delights of the eternal home, the heavenly land that is full of joy. But that hour is not yet come. There remains yet another hour, a time of war, of labor, and of trial. You long to be filled with the highest good, but you cannot attain it now. I am that sovereign Good. Await Me, until the kingdom of God shall come.

You must still be tried on earth, and exercised in many things. Consolation will sometimes be given you, but the complete fullness of it is not granted. Take courage, therefore, and be strong both to do and to suffer what is contrary to nature.

You must put on the new man. You must be changed into another man. You must often do the things you do not wish to do and forego those you do wish. What pleases others will succeed; what pleases you will not. The words of others will be heard; what you say will be accounted as nothing. Others will ask and receive; you will ask and not receive. Others will gain great fame among men; about you nothing will be said. To others the doing of this or that will be entrusted; you will be judged useless. At all this nature will sometimes be sad, and it will be a great thing if you bear this sadness in silence. For in these and many similar ways the faithful servant of the Lord is wont to be tried, to see how far he can deny himself and break himself in all things.

There is scarcely anything in which you so need to die to self as in seeing and suffering things that are against your will, especially when things that are commanded seem inconvenient or useless. Then, because you are under authority, and dare not resist the higher power, it seems hard to submit to the will of another and give up your own opinion entirely.

But consider, my child, the fruit of these labors, how soon they will end and how greatly they will be rewarded, and you will not be saddened by them, but your patience will receive the strongest consolation. For instead of the little will that you now readily give up, you shall always have your will in heaven. There, indeed, you shall find all that you could desire. There you shall have possession of every good without fear of losing it. There shall your will be forever one with Mine. It shall desire nothing outside of Me and nothing for itself. There no one shall oppose you, no one shall complain of you, no one hinder you, and nothing stand in your way. All that you desire will be present there, replenishing your affection and satisfying it to the full. There I shall render you glory for the reproach you have suffered here; for your sorrow I shall give you a garment of praise, and for the lowest place a seat of power forever. There the fruit of glory will appear, the labor of penance rejoice, and humble subjection be gloriously crowned.

Bow humbly, therefore, under the will of all, and do not heed who said this or commanded that. But let it be your special care when something is commanded, or even hinted at, whether by a superior or an inferior or an equal, that you take it in good part and try honestly to perform it. Let one person seek one thing and another something else. Let one glory in this, another in that, and both be praised a thousand times over. But as for you, rejoice neither in one or the other, but only in contempt of yourself and in My pleasure and honor. Let this be your wish: That whether in life or in death God may be glorified in you.

The Fiftieth Chapter

HOW A DESOLATE PERSON OUGHT TO COMMIT HIMSELF INTO THE HANDS OF GOD

THE DISCIPLE

LORD GOD, Holy Father, may You be blessed now and in eternity. For as You will, so is it done; and what You do is good. Let Your servant rejoice in You—not in himself or in any other, for You alone are true joy. You are my hope and my crown. You, O Lord, are my joy and my honor.

What does Your servant possess that he has not received from You, and that without any merit of his own? Yours are all the things which You have given, all the things which You have made.

I am poor and in labors since my youth, and my soul is sorrowful sometimes even to the point of tears. At times, also, my spirit is troubled because of impending sufferings. I long for the joy of peace. Earnestly I beg for the peace of Your children who are fed by You in the light of consolation. If You give peace, if You infuse holy joy, the soul of Your servant shall be filled with holy song and be devout in praising You. But if You withdraw Yourself, as You so very often do, he will not be able to follow the way of Your commandments, but will rather be obliged to strike his breast and bend the knee, because his today is different from yesterday and the day before when Your light shone upon his head and he was protected in the shadow of Your wings from the temptations rushing upon him.

Just Father, ever to be praised, the hour is come for Your servant to be tried. Beloved Father, it is right that in this hour Your servant should suffer something for You. O Father, forever to be honored, the hour which You knew from all eternity is at hand, when for a short time Your servant should be outwardly oppressed, but inwardly should ever live with You.

Let him be a little slighted, let him be humbled, let him fail in the sight of men, let him be afflicted with sufferings and pains, so that he may rise again with You in the dawn of the new light and be glorified in heaven.

Holy Father, You have so appointed and wished it. What has happened is what You commanded. For this is a favor to Your friend, to suffer and be troubled in the world for Your love, no matter how often and by whom You permit it to happen to him.

Nothing happens in the world without Your design and providence, and without cause. It is well for me, O Lord, that You have humbled me, that I may learn the justice of Your judgments and cast away all presumption and haughtiness of heart. It is profitable for me that shame has covered my face that I may look to You rather than to men for consolation. Hereby I have learned also to fear Your inscrutable judgment falling alike upon the just and unjust yet not without equity and justice.

Thanks to You that You have not spared me evils but have bruised me with bitter blows, inflicting sorrows, sending distress without and within. Under heaven there is none to console me except You, my Lord

God, the heavenly Physician of souls, Who wound and heal, Who cast down to hell and raise up again. Your discipline is upon me and Your very rod shall instruct me.

Behold, beloved Father, I am in Your hands. I bow myself under Your correcting chastisement. Strike my back and my neck, that I may bend my crookedness to Your will. Make of me a pious and humble follower, as in Your goodness You are wont to do, that I may walk according to Your every nod. Myself and all that is mine I commit to You to be corrected, for it is better to be punished here than hereafter.

You know all things without exception, and nothing in man's conscience is hidden from You. Coming events You know before they happen, and there is no need for anyone to teach or admonish You of what is being done on earth. You know what will promote my progress, and how much tribulation will serve to cleanse away the rust of vice. Deal with me according to Your good pleasure and do not despise my sinful life, which is known to none so well or so clearly as to You alone.

Grant me, O Lord, the grace to know what should be known, to praise what is most pleasing to You, to esteem that which appears most precious to You, and to abhor what is unclean in Your sight.

Do not allow me to judge according to the light of my bodily eyes, nor to give sentence according to the hearing of ignorant men's ears. But let me distinguish with true judgment between things visible and spiritual, and always seek above all things Your good pleasure. The senses of men often err in their judgments, and the lovers of this world also err in loving only visible things. How is a man the better for being thought greater by men? The deceiver deceives the deceitful, the vain man deceives the vain, the blind deceives the blind, the weak deceives the weak as often as he extols them, and in truth his foolish praise shames them the more. For, as the humble St. Francis says, whatever anyone is in Your sight, that he is and nothing more.

The Fifty-First Chapter

WHEN WE CANNOT ATTAIN TO THE HIGHEST, WE MUST PRACTICE THE HUMBLE WORKS

The Voice of Christ

MY CHILD, you cannot always continue in the more fervent desire of virtue, or remain in the higher stage of contemplation, but because of humanity's sin you must sometimes descend to lower things and bear the burden of this corruptible life, albeit unwillingly and wearily. As long as you wear a mortal body you will suffer weariness and heaviness of heart. You ought, therefore, to bewail in the flesh the burden of the flesh which keeps you from giving yourself unceasingly to spiritual exercises and divine contemplation.

In such condition, it is well for you to apply yourself to humble, outward works and to refresh yourself in good deeds, to await with unshaken confidence My heavenly visitation, patiently to bear your exile and dryness of mind until you are again visited by Me and freed of all anxieties. For I will cause you to forget your labors and to enjoy inward quiet. I will spread before you the open fields of the Scriptures, so that with an open heart you may begin to advance in the way of My commandments. And you will say: the sufferings of this time are not worthy to be compared with the future glory which shall be revealed to us.

The Fifty-Second Chapter

A MAN OUGHT NOT TO CONSIDER HIMSELF WORTHY OF CONSOLATION, BUT RATHER DESERVING OF CHASTISEMENT

THE DISCIPLE

LORD, I am not worthy of Your consolation or of any spiritual visitation. Therefore, You treat me justly when You leave me poor and desolate. For though I could shed a sea of tears, yet I should not be worthy of Your consolation. Hence, I deserve only to be scourged and punished because I have offended You often and grievously, and have sinned greatly in many things. In all justice, therefore, I am not worthy of any consolation.

But You, O gracious and merciful God, Who do not will that Your works should perish, deign to console Your servant beyond all his merit and above human measure, to show the riches of Your goodness toward the vessels of mercy. For Your consolations are not like the words of men.

What have I done, Lord, that You should confer on me any heavenly comfort? I remember that I have done nothing good, but that I have always been prone to sin and slow to amend. That is true. I cannot deny it. If I said otherwise You would stand against me, and there would be no one to defend me. What have I deserved for my sins except hell and everlasting fire?

In truth, I confess that I am deserving of all scorn and contempt.

Neither is it fitting that I should be remembered among Your devoted servants. And although it is hard for me to hear this, yet for truth's sake I will allege my sins against myself, so that I may more easily deserve to beg Your mercy. What shall I say, guilty as I am and full of all confusion? My tongue can say nothing but this alone: "I have sinned, O Lord, I have sinned; have mercy on me and pardon me. Suffer me a little that I may pour out my grief, before I go to that dark land that is covered with the shadow of death."

What do you especially demand of a guilty and wretched sinner, except that he be contrite and humble himself for his sins? In true sorrow and humility of heart hope of forgiveness is born, the troubled conscience is reconciled, grace is found, man is preserved from the wrath to come, and God and the penitent meet with a holy kiss.

To You, O Lord, humble sorrow for sins is an acceptable sacrifice, a sacrifice far sweeter than the perfume of incense. This is also the pleasing ointment which You would have poured upon Your sacred feet, for a contrite and humble heart You have never despised. Here is a place of refuge from the force of the enemy's anger. Here is amended and washed away whatever defilement has been contracted elsewhere.

The Fifty-Third Chapter

GOD'S GRACE IS NOT GIVEN TO THE EARTHLY MINDED

THE VOICE OF CHRIST

MY CHILD, my grace is precious. It does not allow itself to be mixed with external things or with earthly consolations. Cast away all obstacles to grace, therefore, if you wish to receive its infusion.

Seek to retire within yourself. Love to dwell alone with yourself. Seek no man's conversation, but rather pour forth devout prayer to God that you may keep your mind contrite and your heart pure.

Consider the whole world as nothing. Prefer attendance upon God to all outward occupation, for you cannot attend upon Me and at the same time take delight in external things. You must remove yourself from acquaintances and from dear friends, and keep your mind free of all temporal consolation. Thus the blessed Apostle St. Peter begs the faithful of Christ to keep themselves as strangers and pilgrims in the world.[1]

---

[1] I Peter 2:11.

What great confidence at the hour of death shall be his who is not attached to this world by any affection. But the sickly soul does not know what it is to have a heart thus separated from all things, nor does the natural man know the liberty of the spiritual man. Yet, if he truly wishes to be spiritual, he must renounce both strangers and friends, and must beware of no one more than himself.

If you completely conquer yourself, you will more easily subdue all other things. The perfect victory is to triumph over self. For he who holds himself in such subjection that sensuality obeys reason and reason obeys Me in all matters, is truly his own conqueror and master of the world.

Now, if you wish to climb to this high position you must begin like a man, and lay the ax to the root, in order to tear out and destroy any hidden unruly love of self or of earthly goods. From this vice of too much self-love comes almost every other vice that must be uprooted. And when this evil is vanquished, and brought under control, great peace and quiet will follow at once.

But because few labor to die entirely to self, or tend completely away from self, therefore they remain entangled in self, and cannot be lifted in spirit above themselves. But he who desires to walk freely with Me must mortify all his low and inordinate affections, and must not cling with selfish love or desire to any creature.

The Fifty-Fourth Chapter

THE DIFFERENT MOTIONS OF NATURE AND GRACE

THE VOICE OF CHRIST

MY CHILD, pay careful attention to the movements of nature and of grace, for they move in very contrary and subtle ways, and can scarcely be distinguished by anyone except a man who is spiritual and inwardly enlightened. All men, indeed, desire what is good, and strive for what is good in their words and deeds. For this reason the appearance of good deceives many.

Nature is crafty and attracts many, ensnaring and deceiving them while ever seeking itself. But grace walks in simplicity, turns away from all appearance of evil, offers no deceits, and does all purely for God in whom she rests as her last end.

Nature is not willing to die, or to be kept down, or to be overcome. Nor will it subdue itself or be made subject. Grace, on the contrary, strives for mortification of self. She resists sensuality, seeks to be in subjection, longs to be conquered, has no wish to use her own liberty, loves to be held under discipline, and does not desire to rule over anyone, but wishes rather to live, to stand, and to be always under God for Whose sake she is willing to bow humbly to every human creature.

Nature works for its own interest and looks to the profit it can reap from another. Grace does not consider what is useful and advantageous to herself, but rather what is profitable to many. Nature likes to receive honor and reverence, but grace faithfully attributes all honor and glory to God. Nature fears shame and contempt, but grace is happy to suffer reproach for the name of Jesus. Nature loves ease and physical rest. Grace, however, cannot bear to be idle and embraces labor willingly. Nature seeks to possess what is rare and beautiful, abhorring things that are cheap and coarse. Grace, on the contrary, delights in simple, humble things, not despising those that are rough, nor refusing to be clothed in old garments.

Nature has regard for temporal wealth and rejoices in earthly gains. It is sad over a loss and irritated by a slight, injurious word. But grace looks to eternal things and does not cling to those which are temporal, being neither disturbed at loss nor angered by hard words, because she has placed her treasure and joy in heaven where nothing is lost.

Nature is covetous, and receives more willingly than it gives. It loves to have its own private possessions. Grace, however, is kind and open-hearted. Grace shuns private interest, is contented with little, and judges it more blessed to give than to receive.

Nature is inclined toward creatures, toward its own flesh, toward vanities, and toward running about. But grace draws near to God and to virtue, renounces creatures, hates the desires of the flesh, restrains her wanderings and blushes at being seen in public.

Nature likes to have some external comfort in which it can take sensual delight, but grace seeks consolation only in God, to find her delight in the highest Good, above all visible things.

Nature does everything for its own gain and interest. It can do nothing without pay and hopes for its good deeds to receive their equal or better, or else praise and favor. It is very desirous of having its deeds and gifts highly regarded. Grace, however, seeks nothing temporal, nor does she ask any recompense but God alone. Of temporal necessities she asks no more than will serve to obtain eternity.

Nature rejoices in many friends and kinsfolk, glories in noble position and birth, fawns on the powerful, flatters the rich, and applauds those who are like itself. But grace loves even her enemies and is not puffed up at having many friends. She does not think highly of either position or birth unless there is also virtue there. She favors the poor in preference to the rich. She sympathizes with the innocent rather than with the powerful. She rejoices with the true man rather than with the deceitful, and is always exhorting the good to strive for better gifts, to become like the Son of God by practicing the virtues.

Nature is quick to complain of need and trouble; grace is stanch in suffering want.

Nature turns all things back to self. It fights and argues for self. Grace brings all things back to God in Whom they have their source. To herself she ascribes no good, nor is she arrogant or presumptuous. She is not contentious. She does not prefer her own opinion to the opinion of others, but in every matter of sense and thought submits herself to eternal wisdom and the divine judgment.

Nature has a relish for knowing secrets and hearing news. It wishes to appear abroad and to have many sense experiences. It wishes to be known and to do things for which it will be praised and admired. But grace does not care to hear news or curious matters, because all this arises from the old corruption of man, since there is nothing new, nothing lasting on earth. Grace teaches, therefore, restraint of the senses, avoidance of vain self-satisfaction and show, the humble hiding of deeds worthy of praise and admiration, and the seeking in every thing and in every knowledge the fruit of usefulness, the praise and honor of God. She will not have herself or hers exalted, but desires that God Who bestows all simply out of love should be blessed in His gifts.

This grace is a supernatural light, a certain special gift of God, the proper mark of the elect and the pledge of everlasting salvation. It raises man up from earthly things to love the things of heaven. It makes a spiritual man of a carnal one.

The more, then, nature is held in check and conquered, the more grace is given. Every day the interior man is reformed by new visitations according to the image of God.

The Fifty-Fifth Chapter

THE CORRUPTION OF NATURE AND THE EFFICACY OF DIVINE GRACE

THE DISCIPLE

O LORD, my God, Who created me to Your own image and likeness, grant me this grace which You have shown to be so great and necessary for salvation, that I may overcome my very evil nature that is drawing me to sin and perdition. For I feel in my flesh the law of sin contradicting the law of my mind and leading me captive to serve sensuality

in many things. I cannot resist the passions thereof unless Your m[...]
holy grace warmly infused into my heart assist me.

There is need of Your grace, and of great grace, in order to overcome a nature prone to evil from youth. For through the first man, Adam, nature is fallen and weakened by sin, and the punishment of that stain has fallen upon all mankind. Thus nature itself, which You created good and right, is considered a symbol of vice and the weakness of corrupted nature, because when left to itself it tends toward evil and to baser things. The little strength remaining in it is like a spark hidden in ashes. That strength is natural reason which, surrounded by thick darkness, still has the power of judging good and evil, of seeing the difference between true and false, though it is not able to fulfill all that it approves and does not enjoy the full light of truth or soundness of affection.

Hence it is, my God, that according to the inward man I delight in Your law, knowing that Your command is good, just, and holy, and that it proves the necessity of shunning all evil and sin. But in the flesh I keep the law of sin, obeying sensuality rather than reason. Hence, also, it is that the will to good is present in me, but how to accomplish it I know not. Hence, too, I often propose many good things, but because the grace to help my weakness is lacking, I recoil and give up at the slightest resistance. Thus it is that I know the way of perfection and see clearly enough how I ought to act, but because I am pressed down by the weight of my own corruption I do not rise to more perfect things.

How extremely necessary to me, O Lord, Your grace is to begin any good deed, to carry it on and bring it to completion! For without grace I can do nothing, but with its strength I can do all things in You. O Grace truly heavenly, without which our merits are nothing and no gifts of nature are to be esteemed!

Before You, O Lord, no arts or riches, no beauty or strength, no wit or intelligence avail without grace. For the gifts of nature are common to good and bad alike, but the peculiar gift of Your elect is grace or love, and those who are signed with it are held worthy of everlasting life. So excellent is this grace that without it no gift of prophecy or of miracles, no meditation be it ever so exalted, can be considered anything. Not even faith or hope or other virtues are acceptable to You without charity and grace.

O most blessed grace, which makes the poor in spirit rich in virtues, which renders him who is rich in many good things humble of heart, come, descend upon me, fill me quickly with your consolation lest my soul faint with weariness and dryness of mind.

Let me find grace in Your sight, I beg, Lord, for Your grace is enough for me, even though I obtain none of the things which nature desires.

nd afflicted with many tribulations, I will fear no evils
e is with me. This is my strength. This will give me
. This is more powerful than all my enemies and wiser
This is the mistress of truth, the teacher of discipline,
the light of the heart, the consoler in anguish, the banisher of sorrow,
the expeller of fear, the nourisher of devotion, the producer of tears.
What am I without grace, but dead wood, a useless branch, fit only to
be cast away?

Let Your grace, therefore, go before me and follow me, O Lord, and
make me always intent upon good works, through Jesus Christ, Your Son.

The Fifty-Sixth Chapter

WE OUGHT TO DENY OURSELVES AND IMITATE
CHRIST THROUGH BEARING THE CROSS

THE VOICE OF CHRIST

MY CHILD, the more you depart from yourself, the more you will be
able to enter into Me. As the giving up of exterior things brings interior
peace, so the forsaking of self unites you to God. I will have you learn
perfect surrender to My will, without contradiction or complaint.

Follow Me. I am the Way, the Truth, and the Life. Without the Way,
there is no going. Without the Truth, there is no knowing. Without the
Life, there is no living. I am the Way which you must follow, the Truth
which you must believe, the Life for which you must hope. I am the
inviolable Way, the infallible Truth, the unending Life. I am the Way
that is straight, the supreme Truth, the Life that is true, the blessed, the
uncreated Life. If you abide in My Way you shall know the Truth, and
the Truth shall make you free, and you shall attain life everlasting.

If you wish to enter into life, keep My commandments. If you will
know the truth, believe in Me. If you will be perfect, sell all. If you will
be My disciple, deny yourself. If you will possess the blessed life, despise
this present life. If you will be exalted in heaven, humble yourself on
earth. If you wish to reign with Me, carry the Cross with Me. For only the
servants of the Cross find the life of blessedness and of true light.

THE DISCIPLE

Lord Jesus, because Your way is narrow and despised by the world,
grant that I may despise the world and imitate You. For the servant is
not greater than his Lord, nor the disciple above the Master. Let Your

servant be trained in Your life, for there is my salvation and true holiness. Whatever else I read or hear does not fully refresh or delight me.

THE VOICE OF CHRIST

My child, now that you know these things and have read them all, happy will you be if you do them. He who has My commandments and keeps them, he it is that loves Me. And I will love him and will show Myself to him, and will bring it about that he will sit down with Me in My Father's Kingdom.

THE DISCIPLE

Lord Jesus, as You have said, so be it, and what You have promised, let it be my lot to win. I have received the cross, from Your hand I have received it. I will carry it, carry it even unto death as You have laid it upon me. Truly, the life of a good religious man is a cross, but it leads to paradise. We have begun—we may not go back, nor may we leave off.

Take courage, brethren, let us go forward together and Jesus will be with us. For Jesus' sake we have taken this cross. For Jesus' sake let us persevere with it. He will be our help as He is also our leader and guide. Behold, our King goes before us and will fight for us. Let us follow like men. Let no man fear any terrors. Let us be prepared to meet death valiantly in battle. Let us not suffer our glory to be blemished by fleeing from the Cross.

The Fifty-Seventh Chapter

A MAN SHOULD NOT BE TOO DOWNCAST WHEN HE FALLS INTO DEFECTS

THE VOICE OF CHRIST

MY CHILD, patience and humility in adversity are more pleasing to Me than much consolation and devotion when things are going well.

Why are you saddened by some little thing said against you? Even if it had been more you ought not to have been affected. But now let it pass. It is not the first, nor is it anything new, and if you live long it will not be the last.

You are manly enough so long as you meet no opposition. You give good advice to others, and you know how to strengthen them with words, but when unexpected tribulation comes to your door, you fail both in counsel and in strength. Consider your great weakness, then, which you experience so often in small matters. Yet when these and like trials happen, they happen for your good.

Put it out of your heart as best you know how, and if it has touched you, still do not let it cast you down or confuse you for long. Bear it patiently at least, if you cannot bear it cheerfully. Even though you bear it unwillingly, and are indignant at it, restrain yourself and let no ill-ordered words pass your lips at which the weak might be scandalized. The storm that is now aroused will soon be quieted and your inward grief will be sweetened by returning grace. "I yet live," says the Lord, "ready to help you and to console you more and more, if you trust in Me and call devoutly upon Me."

Remain tranquil and prepare to bear still greater trials. All is not lost even though you be troubled oftener or tempted more grievously. You are a man, not God. You are flesh, not an angel. How can you possibly expect to remain always in the same state of virtue when the angels in heaven and the first man in paradise failed to do so? I am He Who rescues the afflicted and brings to My divinity those who know their own weakness.

THE DISCIPLE

Blessed be Your words, O Lord, sweeter to my mouth than honey and the honeycomb. What would I do in such great trials and anxieties, if You did not strengthen me with Your holy words? If I may but attain to the haven of salvation, what does it matter what or how much I suffer? Grant me a good end. Grant me a happy passage out of this world. Remember me, my God, and lead me by the right way into Your kingdom.

The Fifty-Eighth Chapter

HIGH MATTERS AND THE HIDDEN JUDGMENTS OF GOD ARE NOT TO BE SCRUTINIZED

THE VOICE OF CHRIST

MY CHILD, beware of discussing high matters and God's hidden judgments—why this person is so forsaken and why that one is favored with so great a grace, or why one man is so afflicted and another so highly exalted. Such things are beyond all human ken and no reason or disputation can fathom the judgments of God.

When the enemy puts such suggestions in your mind, therefore, or when some curious persons raise questions about them, answer with the prophet: "Thou art just, O Lord, and righteous are Thy judgments";[1] and this: "The judgments of the Lord are true and wholly righteous."[2] My judgments are to be feared, not discussed, because they are incomprehensible to the understanding of men.

In like manner, do not inquire or dispute about the merits of the saints, as to which is more holy, or which shall be greater in the kingdom of heaven. Such things often breed strife and useless contentions. They nourish pride and vainglory, whence arise envy and quarrels, when one proudly tries to exalt one saint and the other another. A desire to know and pry into such matters brings forth no fruit. On the contrary, it displeases the saints, because I am the God, not of dissension, but of peace—of that peace which consists in true humility rather than in self-exaltation.

Some are drawn by the ardor of their love with greater affection to these saints or to those, but this affection is human and not divine. I am He who made all the saints. I gave them grace. I brought them to glory. I know the merits of each of them. I came before them in the blessings of My sweetness. I knew My beloved ones before the ages. I chose them out of the world—they did not choose Me. I called them by grace, I drew them on by mercy. I led them safely through various temptations. I poured into them glorious consolations. I gave them perseverance and I crowned their patience. I know the first and the last. I embrace them all with love inestimable. I am to be praised in all My saints. I am to be blessed above all things, and honored in each of those whom I have exalted and predestined so gloriously without any previous merits of their own.

He who despises one of the least of mine, therefore, does no honor to the greatest, for both the small and the great I made. And he who disparages one of the saints disparages Me also and all others in the kingdom of heaven. They are all one through the bond of charity. They have the same thought and the same will, and they mutually love one another; but, what is a much greater thing, they love Me more than themselves or their own merits. Rapt above themselves, and drawn beyond love of self, they are entirely absorbed in love of Me, in Whom

---

[1] Ps. 118:137.
[2] Ps. 18:10.

they rest. There is nothing that can draw them away or depress them, for they who are filled with eternal truth burn with the fire of unquenchable love.

Therefore, let carnal and sensual men, who know only how to love their own selfish joys, forbear to dispute about the state of God's saints. Such men take away and add according to their own inclinations and not as it pleases the Eternal Truth. In many this is sheer ignorance, especially in those who are but little enlightened and can rarely love anyone with a purely spiritual love. They are still strongly drawn by natural affection and human friendship to one person or another, and on their behavior in such things here below are based their imaginings of heavenly things. But there is an incomparable distance between the things which the imperfect imagine and those which enlightened men contemplate through revelation from above.

Be careful, then, My child, of treating matters beyond your knowledge out of curiosity. Let it rather be your business and aim to be found, even though the least, in the kingdom of God. For though one were to know who is more holy than another, or who is greater in the kingdom of heaven, of what value would this knowledge be to him unless out of it he should humble himself before Me and should rise up in greater praise of My name?

The man who thinks of the greatness of his own sins and the littleness of his virtues, and of the distance between himself and the perfection of the saints, acts much more acceptably to God than the one who argues about who is greater or who is less. It is better to invoke the saints with devout prayers and tears, and with a humble mind to beg their glorious aid, than to search with vain inquisitiveness into their secrets.

The saints are well and perfectly contented if men know how to content themselves and cease their useless discussions. They do not glory in their own merits, for they attribute no good to themselves but all to Me, because out of My infinite charity I gave all to them. They are filled with such love of God and with such overflowing joy, that no glory is wanting to them and they can lack no happiness. All the saints are so much higher in glory as they are more humble in themselves, nearer to Me, and more beloved by Me. Therefore, you find it written that they cast their crowns before God, and fell down upon their faces before the Lamb, and adored Him Who lives forever.

Many ask who is the greater in the kingdom of heaven when they do not know whether they themselves shall be worthy of being numbered among its least. It is a great thing to be even the least in heaven where all are great because all shall be called, and shall be, the children of God. The least shall be as a thousand, and the sinner of a hundred years shall die. For when the disciples asked who should be greater in the kingdom of heaven they heard this response: "Unless you be converted and become as little children, you shall not enter into the kingdom of heaven. Therefore, whosoever shall humble himself as this little child, he is the greater in the kingdom of heaven."[3]

Woe to those, therefore, who disdain to humble themselves willingly with the little children, for the low gate of the heavenly kingdom will not permit them to enter. Woe also to the rich who have their consolations here, for when the poor enter into God's kingdom, they will stand outside lamenting. Rejoice, you humble, and exult, you poor, for the kingdom of God is yours, if only you walk in the truth.

The Fifty-Ninth Chapter

ALL HOPE AND TRUST ARE TO BE FIXED IN GOD ALONE

THE DISCIPLE

WHAT, LORD, is the trust which I have in this life, or what is my greatest comfort among all the things that appear under heaven? Is it not You, O Lord, my God, Whose mercies are without number? Where have I ever fared well but for You? Or how could things go badly when You were present? I had rather be poor for Your sake than rich without You. I prefer rather to wander on the earth with You than to possess heaven without You. Where You are there is heaven, and where You are not are death and hell. You are my desire and therefore I must cry after You and sigh and pray. In none can I fully trust to help me in my necessities, but in You alone, my God. You are my hope. You are my confidence. You are my consoler, most faithful in every need.

All seek their own interests. You, however, place my salvation and my profit first, and turn all things to my good. Even though exposing me to various temptations and hardships, You Who are accustomed to prove Your loved ones in a thousand ways, order all this for my good. You ought not to be loved or praised less in this trial than if You had filled me with heavenly consolations.

In You, therefore, O Lord God, I place all my hope and my refuge. On You I cast all my troubles and anguish, because whatever I have outside of You I find to be weak and unstable. It will not serve me to have many friends, nor will powerful helpers be able to assist me, nor prudent advisers to give useful answers, nor the books of learned men

---

[3] Matt. 18:3, 4.

to console, nor any precious substance to win my freedom, nor any place, secret and beautiful though it be, to shelter me, if You Yourself do not assist, comfort, console, instruct, and guard me. For all things which seem to be for our peace and happiness are nothing when You are absent, and truly confer no happiness.

You, indeed, are the fountain of all good, the height of life, the depth of all that can be spoken. To trust in You above all things is the strongest comfort of Your servants.

My God, the Father of mercies, to You I look, in You I trust. Bless and sanctify my soul with heavenly benediction, so that it may become Your holy dwelling and the seat of Your eternal glory. And in this temple of Your dignity let nothing be found that might offend Your majesty. In Your great goodness, and in the multitude of Your mercies, look upon me and listen to the prayer of Your poor servant exiled from You in the region of the shadow of death. Protect and preserve the soul of Your poor servant among the many dangers of this corruptible life, and direct him by Your accompanying grace, through the ways of peace, to the land of everlasting light.

BOOK FOUR

AN INVITATION TO HOLY COMMUNION

THE VOICE OF CHRIST

COME TO ME, all you that labor and are burdened, and I will refresh you.[1] The bread which I will give is My Flesh, for the life of the world.[2] Take you and eat: this is My Body, which shall be delivered for you. Do this for the commemoration of Me.[3] He that eateth My flesh, and drinketh My blood, abideth in Me, and I in him.[4] The words that I have spoken to you are spirit and life."[5]

The First Chapter

THE GREAT REVERENCE WITH WHICH
WE SHOULD RECEIVE CHRIST

THE DISCIPLE

THESE ARE all Your words, O Christ, eternal Truth, though they were not all spoken at one time nor written together in one place. And because they are Yours and true, I must accept them all with faith and

---

[1] Matt. 11.28.
[2] John 6:52.
[3] I Cor. 11:24.
[4] John 6:57.
[5] John 6:64.

gratitude. They are Yours and You have spoken them; they are mine also because You have spoken them for my salvation. Gladly I accept them from Your lips that they may be the more deeply impressed in my heart.

Words of such tenderness, so full of sweetness and love, encourage me; but my sins frighten me and an unclean conscience thunders at me when approaching such great mysteries as these. The sweetness of Your words invites me, but the multitude of my vices oppresses me.

You command me to approach You confidently if I wish to have part with You, and to receive the food of immortality if I desire to obtain life and glory everlasting.

"Come to me," You say, "all you that labor and are burdened, and I will refresh you."[6]

Oh, how sweet and kind to the ear of the sinner is the word by which You, my Lord God, invite the poor and needy to receive Your most holy Body! Who am I, Lord, that I should presume to approach You? Behold, the heaven of heavens cannot contain You, and yet You say: "Come, all of you, to Me."

What means this most gracious honor and this friendly invitation? How shall I dare to come, I who am conscious of no good on which to presume? How shall I lead You into my house, I who have so often offended in Your most kindly sight? Angels and archangels revere You, the holy and the just fear You, and You say: "Come to Me, all of you!" If You, Lord, had not said it, who would have believed it to be true? And if You had not commanded, who would dare approach?

Behold, Noe, a just man, worked a hundred years building the ark that he and a few others might be saved; how, then, can I prepare myself in one hour to receive with reverence the Maker of the world?

Moses, Your great servant and special friend, made an ark of incorruptible wood which he covered with purest gold wherein to place the tables of Your law; shall I, a creature of corruption, dare so easily to receive You, the Maker of law and the Giver of life?

Solomon, the wisest of the kings of Israel, spent seven years building a magnificent temple in praise of Your name, and celebrated its dedication with a feast of eight days. He offered a thousand victims in Your honor and solemnly bore the Ark of the Covenant with trumpeting and jubilation to the place prepared for it; and I, unhappy and poorest of men, how shall I lead You into my house, I who scarcely can spend a half-hour devoutly—would that I could spend even that as I ought!

O my God, how hard these men tried to please You! Alas, how little is all that I do! How short the time I spend in preparing for Communion!

[6] Matt. 11:28.

I am seldom wholly recollected, and very seldom, indeed, entirely free from distraction. Yet surely in the presence of Your life-giving Godhead no unbecoming thought should arise and no creature possess my heart, for I am about to receive as my guest, not an angel, but the very Lord of angels.

Very great, too, is the difference between the Ark of the Covenant with its treasures and Your most pure Body with its ineffable virtues, between these sacrifices of the law which were but figures of things to come and the true offering of Your Body which was the fulfillment of all ancient sacrifices.

Why, then, do I not long more ardently for Your adorable presence? Why do I not prepare myself with greater care to receive Your sacred gifts, since those holy patriarchs and prophets of old, as well as kings and princes with all their people, have shown such affectionate devotion for the worship of God?

The most devout King David danced before the ark of God with all his strength as he recalled the benefits once bestowed upon his fathers. He made musical instruments of many kinds. He composed psalms and ordered them sung with joy. He himself often played upon the harp when moved by the grace of the Holy Ghost. He taught the people of Israel to praise God with all their hearts and to raise their voices every day to bless and glorify Him. If such great devotion flourished in those days and such ceremony in praise of God before the Ark of the Covenant, what great devotion ought not I and all Christian people now show in the presence of this Sacrament; what reverence in receiving the most excellent Body of Christ!

Many people travel far to honor the relics of the saints, marveling at their wonderful deeds and at the building of magnificent shrines. They gaze upon and kiss the sacred relics encased in silk and gold; and behold, You are here present before me on the altar, my God, Saint of saints, Creator of men, and Lord of angels!

Often in looking at such things, men are moved by curiosity, by the novelty of the unseen, and they bear away little fruit for the amendment of their lives, especially when they go from place to place lightly and without true contrition. But here in the Sacrament of the altar You are wholly present, my God, the man Christ Jesus, whence is obtained the full realization of eternal salvation, as often as You are worthily and devoutly received. To this, indeed, we are not drawn by levity, or curiosity, or sensuality, but by firm faith, devout hope, and sincere love.

O God, hidden Creator of the world, how wonderfully You deal with us! How sweetly and graciously You dispose of things with Your elect to whom You offer Yourself to be received in this Sacrament! This, indeed, surpasses all understanding. This in a special manner attracts the hearts of the devout and inflames their love. Your truly faithful servants, who give their whole life to amendment, often receive in Holy Communion the great grace of devotion and love of virtue.

Oh, the wonderful and hidden grace of this Sacrament which only the faithful of Christ understand, which unbelievers and slaves of sin cannot experience! In it spiritual grace is conferred, lost virtue restored, and the beauty, marred by sin, repaired. At times, indeed, its grace is so great that, from the fullness of the devotion, not only the mind but also the frail body feels filled with greater strength.

Nevertheless, our neglect and coldness is much to be deplored and pitied, when we are not moved to receive with greater fervor Christ in Whom is the hope and merit of all who will be saved. He is our sanctification and redemption. He is our consolation in this life and the eternal joy of the blessed in heaven. This being true, it is lamentable that many pay so little heed to the salutary Mystery which fills the heavens with joy and maintains the whole universe in being.

Oh, the blindness and the hardness of the heart of man that does not show more regard for so wonderful a gift, but rather falls into carelessness from its daily use! If this most holy Sacrament were celebrated in only one place and consecrated by only one priest in the whole world, with what great desire, do you think, would men be attracted to that place, to that priest of God, in order to witness the celebration of the divine Mysteries! But now there are many priests and Mass is offered in many places, that God's grace and love for men may appear the more clearly as the Sacred Communion is spread more widely through the world.

Thanks be to You, Jesus, everlasting Good Shepherd, Who have seen fit to feed us poor exiled people with Your precious Body and Blood, and to invite us with words from Your own lips to partake of these sacred Mysteries: "Come to Me, all you who labor and are burdened, and I will refresh you."

The Second Chapter

GOD'S GREAT GOODNESS AND LOVE IS SHOWN TO MAN IN THIS SACRAMENT

THE DISCIPLE

TRUSTING IN Your goodness and great mercy, O Lord, I come as one sick to the Healer, as one hungry and thirsty to the Fountain of life, as one in need to the King of heaven, a servant to his Lord, a creature to his Creator, a soul in desolation to my gentle Comforter.

But whence is this to me, that You should come to me? Who am I that You should offer Yourself to me? How dares the sinner to appear in Your presence, and You, how do You condescend to come to the sinner? You know Your servant, and You know that he has nothing good in him that You should grant him this.

I confess, therefore, my unworthiness. I acknowledge Your goodness. I praise Your mercy, and give thanks for Your immense love. For it is because of Yourself that You do it, not for any merit of mine; so that Your goodness may be better known to me, that greater love may be aroused and more perfect humility born in me. Since, then, this pleases You and You have so willed it, Your graciousness pleases me also. Oh, that my sinfulness may not stand in the way!

O most sweet and merciful Jesus, what great reverence, thanks, and never-ending praise are due to You for our taking of Your sacred body, whose dignity no man can express!

But on what shall I think in this Communion, this approach to my Lord, Whom I can never reverence as I ought, and yet Whom I desire devoutly to receive? What thought better, more helpful to me than to humble myself entirely in Your presence and exalt Your infinite goodness above myself?

I praise You, my God, and extol You forever! I despise myself and cast myself before You in the depths of my unworthiness. Behold, You are the Holy of holies, and I the scum of sinners! Behold, You bow down to me who am not worthy to look up to You! Behold, You come to me! You will to be with me! You invite me to Your banquet! You desire to give me heavenly food, the Bread of Angels to eat, none other than Yourself, the living Bread Who are come down from heaven and give life to the world.

Behold, whence love proceeds! What condescension shines forth! What great thanks and praise are due You for these gifts! Oh, how salutary and profitable was Your design in this institution! How sweet and pleasant the banquet when You gave Yourself as food!

How admirable is Your work, O Lord! How great Your power! How infallible Your truth! For You spoke and all things were made, and this, which You commanded, was done. It is a wonderful thing, worthy of faith, overpowering human understanding, that You, O Lord, my God, true God and man, are contained whole and entire under the appearance of a little bread and wine, and without being consumed are eaten by him who receives You!

You, the Lord of the universe, Who have need of nothing, have willed to dwell in us by means of Your Sacrament. Keep my heart and body clean, so that with a joyous and spotless conscience I may be able often to celebrate Your Mysteries and to receive for my eternal salvation what You have ordained and instituted for Your special honor and as an everlasting memorial.

Rejoice, my soul, and give thanks to God for having left you so noble a gift and so special a consolation in this valley of tears. As often as you renew this Mystery and receive the Body of Christ, so often do you enact the work of redemption and become a sharer in all the merits of Christ, for the love of Christ never grows less and the wealth of His mercy is never exhausted.

Therefore, you should prepare yourself for it by constantly renewing your heart and pondering deeply the great mystery of salvation. As often as you celebrate or hear Mass, it should seem as great, as new, as sweet to you as if on that very day Christ became man in the womb of the Virgin, or, hanging on the Cross, suffered and died for the salvation of man.

The Third Chapter

IT IS PROFITABLE TO RECEIVE COMMUNION OFTEN

THE DISCIPLE

BEHOLD, I come to You, Lord, that I may prosper by Your gift and be delighted at Your holy banquet which You, O God, in Your sweetness have prepared for Your poor. Behold, all that I can or ought to desire is in You. You are my salvation and my redemption, my hope and strength, my honor and glory.

Gladden, then, this day the soul of Your servant because I have raised my heart to You, O Lord Jesus. I long to receive You now, devoutly and reverently. I desire to bring You into my house that, with Zacheus, I may merit Your blessing and be numbered among the children of Abraham.

My soul longs for Your Body; my heart desires to be united with You. Give me Yourself—it is enough; for without You there is no consolation. Without You I cannot exist, without Your visitation I cannot live. I must often come to You, therefore, and receive the strength of my salvation lest, deprived of this heavenly food, I grow weak on the way. Once, most merciful Jesus, while preaching to the people and healing their many ills, You said: "I will not send them away fasting, lest they faint in the way."[1] Deal with me likewise, You Who have left Yourself in this Sacrament for the consolation of the faithful. You are sweet

---

[1] Matt. 15:32.

refreshment to the soul, and he who eats You worthily will be a sharer in, and an heir to, eternal glory.

It is indeed necessary for me, who fall and sin so often, who so quickly become lax and weak, to renew, cleanse, and inflame myself through frequent prayer, confession, and the holy reception of Your Body, lest perhaps by abstaining too long, I fall away from my holy purpose. For from the days of his youth the senses of man are prone to evil, and unless divine aid strengthens him, he quickly falls deeper. But Holy Communion removes him from evil and confirms him in good.

If I am so often careless and lax when I celebrate or communicate, what would happen if I did not receive this remedy and seek so great a help? Although I am neither fit nor properly disposed to celebrate every day, yet I will do my best at proper times to receive the divine Mysteries and share in this great grace. This, indeed, is the one chief consolation of the faithful soul when separated from You by mortality, that often mindful of her God, she receives her Beloved with devout recollection.

Oh, wonderful condescension of Your affection toward us, that You, the Lord God, Creator and Giver of life to all, should see fit to come to a poor soul and to appease her hunger with all Your divinity and humanity! O happy mind and blessed soul which deserves to receive You, her Lord God, and in receiving You, is filled with spiritual joy! How great a Master she entertains, what a beloved guest she receives, how sweet a companion she welcomes, how true a friend she gains, how beautiful and noble is the spouse she embraces, beloved and desired above all things that can be loved and desired! Let heaven and earth and all their treasures stand silent before Your face, most sweetly Beloved, for whatever glory and beauty they have is of Your condescending bounty, and they cannot approach the beauty of Your name, Whose wisdom is untold.

The Fourth Chapter

MANY BLESSINGS ARE GIVEN THOSE WHO RECEIVE COMMUNION WORTHILY

THE DISCIPLE

O LORD my God, favor Your servant with the blessings of Your sweetness that I may merit to approach Your magnificent Sacrament worthily and devoutly. Lift up my heart to You and take away from me this heavy indolence. Visit me with Your saving grace that I may in spirit taste Your sweetness which lies hidden in this Sacrament like water in the depths of a spring. Enlighten my eyes to behold this great Mystery, and give me strength to believe in it with firm faith.

For it is Your work, not the power of man, Your sacred institution, not his invention. No man is able of himself to comprehend and understand these things which surpass even the keen vision of angels. How, then, shall I, an unworthy sinner who am but dust and ashes, be able to fathom and understand so great a mystery?

O Lord, I come to You at Your command in simplicity of heart, in good, firm faith, with hope and reverence, and I truly believe that You are present here in this Sacrament, God and man. It is Your will that I receive You and unite myself to You in love. Wherefore, I beg Your mercy and ask that special grace be given me, that I may be wholly dissolved in You and filled with Your love, no longer to concern myself with exterior consolations. For this, the highest and most worthy Sacrament, is the health of soul and body, the cure of every spiritual weakness. In it my defects are remedied, my passions restrained, and temptations overcome or allayed. In it greater grace is infused, growing virtue is nourished, faith confirmed, hope strengthened, and charity fanned into flame.

You, my God, the protector of my soul, the strength of human weakness, and the giver of every interior consolation, have given and still do often give in this Sacrament great gifts to Your loved ones who communicate devoutly. Moreover, You give them many consolations amid their numerous troubles and lift them from the depths of dejection to the hope of Your protection. With new graces You cheer and lighten them within, so that they who are full of anxiety and without affection before Communion may find themselves changed for the better after partaking of this heavenly food and drink.

Likewise, You so deal with Your elect that they may truly acknowledge and plainly experience how weak they are in themselves and what goodness and grace they obtain from You. For though in themselves they are cold, obdurate, and wanting in devotion, through You they become fervent, cheerful, and devout.

Who, indeed, can humbly approach the fountain of sweetness and not carry away a little of it? Or who, standing before a blazing fire does not feel some of its heat? You are a fountain always filled with superabundance! You are a fire, ever burning, that never fails!

Therefore, while I may not exhaust the fullness of the fountain or drink to satiety, yet will I put my lips to the mouth of this heavenly stream that from it I may receive at least some small drop to refresh my thirst and not wither away. And if I cannot as yet be all heavenly or as full of fire as the cherubim and seraphim, yet I will try to become more devout and prepare my heart so that I may gather some small spark of divine fire from the humble reception of this life-giving Sacrament.

Whatever is wanting in me, good Jesus, Saviour most holy, do You in Your kindness and grace supply for me, You Who have been pleased to call all unto You, saying: "Come to Me all you that labor and are burdened and I will refresh you."

I, indeed, labor in the sweat of my brow. I am torn with sorrow of heart. I am laden with sin, troubled with temptations, enmeshed and oppressed by many evil passions, and there is none to help me, none to deliver and save me but You, my Lord God and Saviour, to Whom I entrust myself and all I have, that You may protect me and lead me to eternal life. For the honor and glory of Your name receive me, You Who have prepared Your Body and Blood as food and drink for me. Grant, O Lord, my God and Saviour, that by approaching Your Mysteries frequently, the zeal of my devotion may increase.

The Fifth Chapter

THE DIGNITY OF THE SACRAMENT AND OF THE PRIESTHOOD

THE VOICE OF CHRIST

HAD YOU the purity of an angel and the sanctity of St. John the Baptist, you would not be worthy to receive or administer this Sacrament. It is not because of any human meriting that a man consecrates and administers the Sacrament of Christ, and receives the Bread of Angels for his food. Great is the Mystery and great the dignity of priests to whom is given that which has not been granted the angels. For priests alone, rightly ordained in the Church, have power to celebrate Mass and consecrate the Body of Christ.

The priest, indeed, is the minister of God, using the word of God according to His command and appointment. God, moreover, is there—the chief Author and invisible Worker to Whom all is subject as He wills, to Whom all are obedient as He commands.

In this most excellent Sacrament, therefore, you ought to believe in God rather than in your own senses or in any visible sign, and thus, with fear and reverence draw near to such a work as this. Look to yourself and see whose ministry has been given you through the imposition of the bishop's hands.

Behold, you have been made a priest, consecrated to celebrate Mass! See to it now that you offer sacrifice to God faithfully and devoutly at proper times, and that you conduct yourself blamelessly. You have not made your burden lighter. Instead, you are now bound by stricter discipline and held to more perfect sanctity.

A priest ought to be adorned with all virtues and show the example of a good life to others. His way lies not among the vulgar and common habits of men but with the angels in heaven and the perfect men on earth. A priest clad in the sacred vestments acts in Christ's place, that he may pray to God both for himself and for all people in a suppliant and humble manner. He has before and behind him the sign of the Lord's cross that he may always remember the Passion of Christ. It is before him, on the chasuble, that he may look closely upon the footsteps of Christ and try to follow them fervently. It is behind him—he is signed with it—that he may gladly suffer for God any adversities inflicted by others.

He wears the cross before him that he may mourn his own sins, behind him, that in pity he may mourn the sins of others, and know that he is appointed to stand between God and the sinner, never to become weary of prayer and the holy offering until it is granted him to obtain grace and mercy.

When the priest celebrates Mass, he honors God, gladdens the angels, strengthens the Church, helps the living, brings rest to the departed, and wins for himself a share in all good things.

The Sixth Chapter

AN INQUIRY ON THE PROPER THING TO DO BEFORE COMMUNION

THE DISCIPLE

WHEN I consider Your dignity, O Lord, and my own meanness, I become very much frightened and confused. For if I do not receive, I fly from Life, and if I intrude unworthily, I incur Your displeasure. What, then, shall I do, my God, my Helper and Adviser in necessity? Teach me the right way. Place before me some short exercise suitable for Holy Communion, for it is good to know in what manner I ought to make my heart ready devoutly and fervently for You, to receive Your Sacrament for the good of my soul, or even to celebrate so great and divine a sacrifice.

The Seventh Chapter

THE EXAMINATION OF CONSCIENCE AND THE RESOLUTION TO AMEND

THE VOICE OF CHRIST

ABOVE ALL, God's priest should approach the celebration and reception of this Sacrament with the deepest humility of heart and suppliant reverence, with complete faith and the pious intention of giving honor to God.

Carefully examine your conscience, then. Cleanse and purify it to the best of your power by true contrition and humble confession, that you may have no burden, know of no remorse, and thus be free to come near. Let the memory of all your sins grieve you, and especially lament and bewail your daily transgressions. Then if time permits, confess to God in the secret depths of your heart all the miseries your passions have caused.

Lament and grieve because you are still so worldly, so carnal, so passionate and unmortified, so full of roving lust, so careless in guarding the external senses, so often occupied in many vain fancies, so inclined to exterior things and so heedless of what lies within, so prone to laughter and dissipation and so indisposed to sorrow and tears, so inclined to ease and the pleasures of the flesh and so cool to austerity and zeal, so curious to hear what is new and to see the beautiful and so slow to embrace humiliation and dejection, so covetous of abundance, so niggardly in giving and so tenacious in keeping, so inconsiderate in speech, so reluctant in silence, so undisciplined in character, so disordered in action, so greedy at meals, so deaf to the Word of God, so prompt to rest and so slow to labor, so awake to empty conversation, so sleepy in keeping sacred vigils and so eager to end them, so wandering in your attention, so careless in saying the office, so lukewarm in celebrating, so heartless in receiving, so quickly distracted, so seldom fully recollected, so quickly moved to anger, so apt to take offense at others, so prone to judge, so severe in condemning, so happy in prosperity and so weak in adversity, so often making good resolutions and carrying so few of them into action.

When you have confessed and deplored these and other faults with sorrow and great displeasure because of your weakness, be firmly determined to amend your life day by day and to advance in goodness.

Then, with complete resignation and with your entire will offer yourself upon the altar of your heart as an everlasting sacrifice to the honor of My name, by entrusting with faith both body and soul to My care, that thus you may be considered worthy to draw near and offer sacrifice to God and profitably receive the Sacrament of My Body. For there is no more worthy offering, no greater satisfaction for washing away sin than to offer yourself purely and entirely to God with the offering of the Body of Christ in Mass and Communion.

If a man does what he can and is truly penitent, however often he comes to Me for grace and pardon, "As I live, saith the Lord God, I desire not the death of the wicked, but that the wicked turn from his way and live";[1] I will no longer remember his sins, but all will be forgiven him.

The Eighth Chapter

THE OFFERING OF CHRIST ON THE CROSS; OUR OFFERING

THE VOICE OF CHRIST

As I offered Myself willingly to God the Father for your sins with hands outstretched and body naked on the cross, so that nothing remained in Me that had not become a complete sacrifice to appease the divine wrath, so ought you to be willing to offer yourself to Me day by day in the Mass as a pure and holy oblation, together with all your faculties and affections, with as much inward devotion as you can.

What more do I ask than that you give yourself entirely to Me? I care not for anything else you may give Me, for I seek not your gift but you. Just as it would not be enough for you to have everything if you did not have Me, so whatever you give cannot please Me if you do not give yourself.

Offer yourself to Me, therefore, and give yourself entirely for God—your offering will be accepted. Behold, I offered Myself wholly to the Father for you, I even gave My whole Body and Blood for food that I might be all yours, and you Mine forever.

But if you rely upon self, and do not offer your free will to Mine, your offering will be incomplete and the union between us imperfect. Hence, if you desire to attain grace and freedom of heart, let the free

---

[1] Ezek. 33:11.

offering of yourself into the hands of God precede your every action. This is why so few are inwardly free and enlightened — they know not how to renounce themselves entirely.

My word stands: "Everyone of you that doth not renounce all that he possesseth, cannot be My disciple."[1]

If, therefore, you wish to be My disciple, offer yourself to Me with all your heart.

The Ninth Chapter

WE SHOULD OFFER OURSELVES AND ALL THAT WE HAVE TO GOD, PRAYING FOR ALL

THE DISCIPLE

ALL THINGS in heaven and on earth, O Lord, are Yours. I long to give myself to You as a voluntary offering to remain forever Yours. With a sincere heart I offer myself this day to You, O Lord, to Your eternal service, to Your homage, and as a sacrifice of everlasting praise. Receive me with this holy offering of Your precious Body which also I make to You this day, in the presence of angels invisibly attending, for my salvation and that of all Your people.

O Lord, upon Your altar of expiation, I offer You all the sins and offenses I have committed in Your presence and in the presence of Your holy angels, from the day when I first could sin until this hour, that You may burn and consume them all in the fire of Your love, that You may wipe away their every stain, cleanse my conscience of every fault, and restore to me Your grace which I lost in sin by granting full pardon for all and receiving me mercifully with the kiss of peace.

What can I do for all my sins but humbly confess and lament them, and implore Your mercy without ceasing? In Your mercy, I implore You, hear me when I stand before You, my God. All my sins are most displeasing to me. I wish never to commit them again. I am sorry for them and will be sorry as long as I live. I am ready to do penance and make satisfaction to the utmost of my power.

Forgive me, O God, forgive me my sins for Your Holy Name. Save my soul which You have redeemed by Your most precious Blood. See, I place myself at Your mercy. I commit myself to Your hands. Deal with

---

[1] Luke 14:33.

me according to Your goodness, not according to my malicious and evil ways.

I offer to You also all the good I have, small and imperfect though it be, that You may make it more pure and more holy, that You may be pleased with it, render it acceptable to Yourself, and perfect it more and more, and finally that You may lead me, an indolent and worthless creature, to a good and happy end.

I offer You also all the holy desires of Your devoted servants, the needs of my parents, friends, brothers, sisters, and all who are dear to me; of all who for Your sake have been kind to me or to others; of all who have wished and asked my prayers and Masses for them and theirs, whether they yet live in the flesh or are now departed from this world, that they may all experience the help of Your grace, the strength of Your consolation, protection from dangers, deliverance from punishment to come, and that, free from all evils, they may gladly give abundant thanks to You.

I offer You also these prayers and the Sacrifice of Propitiation for those especially who have in any way injured, saddened, or slandered me, inflicted loss or pain upon me, and also for all those whom I have at any time saddened, disturbed, offended, and abused by word or deed, willfully or in ignorance. May it please You to forgive us all alike our sins and offenses against one another.

Take away from our hearts, O Lord, all suspicion, anger, wrath, contention, and whatever may injure charity and lessen brotherly love. Have mercy, O Lord, have mercy on those who ask Your mercy, give grace to those who need it, and make us such that we may be worthy to enjoy Your favor and gain eternal life.

The Tenth Chapter

DO NOT LIGHTLY FOREGO HOLY COMMUNION

The Voice of Christ

You must often return to the source of grace and divine mercy, to the fountain of goodness and perfect purity, if you wish to be free from passion and vice, if you desire to be made stronger and more watchful against all the temptations and deceits of the devil.

The enemy, knowing the great good and the healing power of Holy Communion, tries as much as he can by every manner and means to hinder and keep away the faithful and the devout. Indeed, there are some who suffer the worst assaults of Satan when disposing themselves to prepare for Holy Communion. As it is written in Job, this wicked spirit comes among the sons of God to trouble them by his wonted malice, to make them unduly fearful and perplexed, that thus he may lessen their devotion or attack their faith to such an extent that they perhaps either forego Communion altogether or receive with little fervor.

No attention, however, must be paid to his cunning wiles, no matter how base and horrible — all his suggestions must be cast back upon his head. The wretch is to be despised and scorned. Holy Communion must not be passed by because of any assaults from him or because of the commotion he may arouse.

Oftentimes, also, too great solicitude for devotion and anxiety about confession hinder a person. Do as wise men do. Cast off anxiety and scruple, for it impedes the grace of God and destroys devotion of the mind.

Do not remain away from Holy Communion because of a small trouble or vexation but go at once to confession and willingly forgive all others their offenses. If you have offended anyone, humbly seek pardon and God will readily forgive you.

What good is it to delay confession for a long time or to put off Holy Communion? Cleanse yourself at once, spit out the poison quickly. Make haste to apply the remedy and you will find it better than if you had waited a long time. If you put it off today because of one thing, perhaps tomorrow a greater will occur to you, and thus you will stay away from Communion for a long time and become even more unfit.

Shake off this heaviness and sloth as quickly as you can, for there is no gain in much anxiety, in enduring long hours of trouble, and in depriving yourself of the divine Mysteries because of these daily disturbances. Yes, it is very hurtful to defer Holy Communion long, for it usually brings on a lazy spiritual sleep.

How sad that some dissolute and lax persons are willing to postpone confession and likewise wish to defer Holy Communion, lest they be forced to keep a stricter watch over themselves! Alas, how little love and devotion have they who so easily put off Holy Communion!

How happy and acceptable to God is he who so lives, and keeps his conscience so pure, as to be ready and well disposed to communicate, even every day if he were permitted, and if he could do so unnoticed.

If, now and then, a man abstains by the grace of humility or for a legitimate reason, his reverence is commendable, but if laziness takes hold of him, he must arouse himself and do everything in his power, for the Lord will quicken his desire because of the good intention to which He particularly looks. When he is indeed unable to come, he will always have the good will and pious intention to communicate and thus he will not lose the fruit of the Sacrament.

Any devout person may at any hour on any day receive Christ in spiritual communion profitably and without hindrance. Yet on certain days and times appointed he ought to receive with affectionate reverence the Body of his Redeemer in this Sacrament, seeking the praise and honor of God rather than his own consolation.

For as often as he devoutly calls to mind the mystery and passion of the Incarnate Christ, and is inflamed with love for Him, he communicates mystically and is invisibly refreshed.

He who prepares himself only when festivals approach or custom demands, will often find himself unprepared. Blessed is he who offers himself a holocaust to the Lord as often as he celebrates or communicates.

Be neither too slow nor too fast in celebrating but follow the good custom common to those among whom you are. You ought not to cause others inconvenience or trouble, but observe the accepted rule as laid down by superiors, and look to the benefit of others rather than to your own devotion or inclination.

The Eleventh Chapter

THE BODY OF CHRIST AND SACRED SCRIPTURE ARE MOST NECESSARY TO A FAITHFUL SOUL

THE DISCIPLE

O MOST sweet Lord Jesus, how great is the happiness of the devout soul that feasts upon You at Your banquet, where there is set before her to be eaten no other food but Yourself alone, her only Lover, most desired of all that her heart can desire!

To me it would be happiness, indeed, to shed tears in Your presence from the innermost depths of love, and like the pious Magdalen to wash Your feet with them. But where now is this devotion, this copious shedding of holy tears? Certainly in Your sight, before Your holy angels, my whole heart ought to be inflamed and weep for joy. For, hidden though You are beneath another form, I have You truly present in the Sacrament.

My eyes could not bear to behold You in Your own divine brightness, nor could the whole world stand in the splendor of the glory of Your majesty. In veiling Yourself in the Sacrament, therefore, You have regard for my weakness.

In truth, I possess and adore Him Whom the angels adore in heaven—I as yet by faith, they face to face unveiled. I must be content with the light of the true faith and walk in it until the day of eternal brightness dawns and the shadow of figures passes away. When, moreover, that which is perfect shall have come, the need of sacraments shall cease, for the blessed in heavenly glory need no healing sacrament. Rejoicing endlessly in the presence of God, beholding His glory face to face, transformed from their own brightness to the brightness of the ineffable Deity, they taste the Word of God made flesh, as He was in the beginning and will remain in eternity.

Though mindful of these wonderful things, every spiritual solace becomes wearisome to me because so long as I do not plainly see the Lord in His glory, I consider everything I hear and see on earth of little account.

You are my witness, O God, that nothing can comfort me, no creature give me rest but You, my God, Whom I desire to contemplate forever. But this is not possible while I remain in mortal life, and, therefore, I must be very patient and submit myself to You in every desire.

Even Your saints, O Lord, who now rejoice with You in the kingdom of heaven, awaited the coming of Your glory with faith and great patience while they lived. What they believed, I believe. What they hoped for, I hope for, and whither they arrived, I trust I shall come by Your grace. Meanwhile I will walk in faith, strengthened by the example of the saints. I shall have, besides, for comfort and for the guidance of my life, the holy Books, and above all these, Your most holy Body for my special haven and refuge.

I feel there are especially necessary for me in this life two things without which its miseries would be unbearable. Confined here in this prison of the body I confess I need these two, food and light. Therefore, You have given me in my weakness Your sacred Flesh to refresh my soul and body, and You have set Your word as the guiding light for my feet. Without them I could not live aright, for the word of God is the light of my soul and Your Sacrament is the Bread of Life.

These also may be called the two tables, one here, one there, in the treasure house of holy Church. One is the table of the holy altar, having the holy Bread that is the precious Body of Christ. The other is the table of divine law, containing holy doctrine that teaches all the true faith and firmly leads them within the veil, the Holy of holies.

Thanks to You, Lord Jesus, Light of eternal light, for the table of Your holy teaching which You have prepared for us by Your servants, the prophets and Apostles and other learned men.

Thanks to You, Creator and Redeemer of men, Who, to declare Your love to all the world, have prepared a great supper in which You have placed before us as food not the lamb, the type of Yourself, but Your own most precious Body and Blood, making all the faithful glad in Your sacred banquet, intoxicating them with the chalice of salvation in which are all the delights of paradise; and the holy angels feast with us but with more happiness and sweetness.

Oh, how great and honorable is the office of the priest to whom is given the consecration of the Lord of majesty in sacred words, whose lips bless Him, whose hands hold Him, whose tongue receives Him, and whose ministry it is to bring Him to others!

Oh, how clean those hands should be, how pure the lips, how sanctified the body, how immaculate the heart of the priest to whom the Author of all purity so often comes. No word but what is holy, none but what is good and profitable ought to come from the lips of the priest who so often receives the Sacrament of Christ. Single and modest should be the eyes accustomed to looking upon the Body of Christ. Pure and lifted up to heaven the hands accustomed to handle the Creator of heaven and earth.

To priests above all it is written in the law: "Be ye holy, for I, the Lord your God, am holy."

Let Your grace, almighty God, assist us, that we who have undertaken the office of the priesthood may serve You worthily and devoutly in all purity and with a good conscience. And if we cannot live as innocently as we ought, grant us at least to lament duly the wrongs we have committed and in the spirit of humility and the purpose of a good will to serve You more fervently in the future.

The Twelfth Chapter

THE COMMUNICANT SHOULD PREPARE HIMSELF FOR CHRIST WITH GREAT CARE

THE VOICE OF CHRIST

I AM the Lover of purity, the Giver of all holiness. I seek a pure heart and there is the place of My rest.

Prepare for Me a large room furnished and I with My disciples will keep the Pasch with you.

If you wish that I come to you and remain with you, purge out the old leaven and make clean the dwelling of your heart. Shut out the whole world with all the din of its vices. Sit as the sparrow lonely on the housetop, and think on your transgressions in bitterness of soul.

Everyone who loves prepares the best and most beautiful home for his beloved, because the love of the one receiving his lover is recognized thereby.

But understand that you cannot by any merit of your own make this preparation well enough, though you spend a year in doing it and think of nothing else. It is only by My goodness and grace that you are allowed to approach My table, as though a beggar were invited to dinner by a rich man and he had nothing to offer in return for the gift but to humble himself and give thanks.

Do what you can and do that carefully. Receive the Body of the Lord, your beloved God Who deigns to come to you, not out of habit or necessity, but with fear, with reverence, and with love.

I am He that called you. I ordered it done. I will supply what you lack. Come and receive Me.

When I grant the grace of devotion, give thanks to God, not because you are worthy but because I have had mercy upon you. If you have it not and feel rather dry instead, continue in prayer, sigh and knock, and do not give up until you receive some crumb of saving grace.

You have need of Me. I do not need you. You do not come to sanctify Me but I come to sanctify you and make you better. You come to be sanctified and united with Me, to receive new grace and to be aroused anew to amend. Do not neglect this grace, but prepare your heart with all care, and bring into it your Beloved.

Not only should you prepare devoutly before Communion, but you should also carefully keep yourself in devotion after receiving the Sacrament. The careful custody of yourself afterward is no less necessary than the devout preparation before, for a careful afterwatch is the best preparation for obtaining greater grace. If a person lets his mind wander to external comforts, he becomes quite indisposed.

Beware of much talking. Remain in seclusion and enjoy your God, for you have Him Whom all the world cannot take from you.

I am He to Whom you should give yourself entirely, that from now on you may live, not in yourself, but in Me, with all cares cast away.

The Thirteenth Chapter

WITH ALL HER HEART THE DEVOUT SOUL SHOULD DESIRE UNION WITH CHRIST IN THE SACRAMENT

THE DISCIPLE

LET IT be granted me to find You alone, O Christ, to open to You my whole heart, to enjoy You as my soul desires, to be disturbed by no one, to be moved and troubled by no creature, that You may speak to me and I to You alone, as a lover speaks to his loved one, and friend converses with friend.

I pray for this, I desire this, that I may be completely united to You and may withdraw my heart from all created things, learning to relish the celestial and the eternal through Holy Communion and the frequent celebration of Mass.

Ah Lord God, when shall I be completely united to You and absorbed by You, with self utterly forgotten? You in me and I in You? Grant that we may remain so together. You in truth are my Beloved, chosen from thousands, in Whom my soul is happy to dwell all the days of her life. You are in truth my pledge of peace, in Whom is the greatest peace and true rest, without Whom there is toil and sorrow and infinite misery.

You truly are the hidden God. Your counsel is not with the wicked, and Your conversation is rather with the humble and the simple.

O how kind is Your spirit, Lord, Who in order to show Your sweetness toward Your children, deign to feed them with the sweetest of bread, bread come down from heaven! Surely there is no other people so fortunate as to have their god near them, as You, our God, are present everywhere to the faithful to whom You give Yourself to be eaten and enjoyed for their daily solace and the raising of their hearts to heaven.

Indeed, what other nation is so renowned as the Christian peoples? What creature under heaven is so favored as the devout soul to whom God comes, to feed her with His glorious Flesh? O unspeakable grace! O wonderful condescension! O love beyond measure, singularly bestowed upon man!

What return shall I make to the Lord for this love, this grace so boundless? There is nothing I can give more pleasing than to offer my heart completely to my God, uniting it closely with His. Then shall all my inner self be glad when my soul is perfectly united with God. Then will He say to me: "If you will be with Me, I will be with you." And I will answer Him: "Deign, O Lord, to remain with me. I will gladly be with You. This is my one desire, that my heart may be united with You."

The Fourteenth Chapter

THE ARDENT LONGING OF DEVOUT MEN FOR THE BODY OF CHRIST

THE DISCIPLE

HOW GREAT is the abundance of Your kindness, O Lord, which You have hidden from those who fear You!

When I think how some devout persons come to Your Sacrament with the greatest devotion and love, I am frequently ashamed and confused that I approach Your altar and the table of Holy Communion so coldly and indifferently; that I remain so dry and devoid of heartfelt affection; that I am not completely inflamed in Your presence, O my God, nor so strongly drawn and attracted as many devout persons who, in their great desire for Communion and intense heart love, could not restrain their tears but longed from the depths of their souls and bodies to embrace You, the Fountain of Life. These were able to appease and allay their hunger in no other way than by receiving Your Body with all joy and spiritual eagerness. The faith of these men was true and ardent—convincing proof of Your sacred presence. They whose hearts burn so ardently within them when Jesus lives with them truly know their Lord in the breaking of bread.

Such affection and devotion, such mighty love and zeal are often far beyond me. Be merciful to me, O sweet, good, kind Jesus, and grant me, Your poor suppliant, sometimes at least to feel in Holy Communion a little of the tenderness of Your love, that my faith may grow stronger, that my hope in Your goodness may increase, and that charity, once perfectly kindled within me by tasting heavenly manna, may never fail.

Your mercy can give me the grace I long for and can visit me most graciously with fervor of soul according to Your good pleasure. For although I am not now inflamed with as great desire as those who are singularly devoted to You, yet by Your grace I long for this same great flame, praying and seeking a place among all such ardent lovers that I may be numbered among their holy company.

The Fifteenth Chapter

THE GRACE OF DEVOTION IS ACQUIRED THROUGH HUMILITY AND SELF-DENIAL

THE VOICE OF CHRIST

YOU MUST seek earnestly the grace of devotion, ask for it fervently, await it patiently and hopefully, receive it gratefully, guard it humbly, cooperate with it carefully and leave to God, when it comes, the length and manner of the heavenly visitation.

When you feel little or no inward devotion, you should especially humiliate yourself, but do not become too dejected or unreasonably sad. In one short moment God often gives what He has long denied. At times He grants at the end what He has denied from the beginning of prayer. If grace were always given at once, or were present at our beck and call, it would not be well taken by weak humankind. Therefore, with good hope and humble patience await the grace of devotion.

When it is not given, or for some unknown reason is taken away, blame yourself and your sins. Sometimes it is a small matter that hinders grace and hides it, if, indeed, that which prevents so great a good may be called little rather than great. But if you remove this hindrance, be it great or small, and if you conquer it perfectly, you shall have what you ask. As soon as you have given yourself to God with all your heart and seek neither this nor that for your own pleasure and purpose, but place yourself completely in His charge, you shall find yourself at peace, united with Him, because nothing will be so sweet, nothing will please you so much as the good pleasure of His will.

Anyone, therefore, who shall with simplicity of heart direct his intention to God and free himself from all inordinate love or dislike for any creature will be most fit to receive grace and will be worthy of the gift of devotion. For where the Lord finds the vessel empty He pours down His blessing.

So also the more perfectly a man renounces things of this world, and the more completely he dies to himself through contempt of self, the more quickly this great grace comes to him, the more plentifully it enters in, and the higher it uplifts the free heart.

Then shall he see and abound, then shall his heart marvel and be enlarged within him, because the Hand of the Lord is with him and in the hollow of that Hand he has placed himself forever. Thus shall the man be blessed who seeks God with all his heart and has not regarded his soul in vain. Such a one, receiving the Holy Eucharist, merits the grace of divine union because he looks not on his own thoughts, nor to his own comfort, but above all devotion and consolation to the glory and honor of God.

The Sixteenth Chapter

WE SHOULD SHOW OUR NEEDS TO CHRIST AND ASK HIS GRACE

THE DISCIPLE

O MOST kind, most loving Lord, Whom I now desire to receive with devotion, You know the weakness and the necessity which I suffer, in what great evils and vices I am involved, how often I am depressed, tempted, defiled, and troubled.

To You I come for help, to You I pray for comfort and relief. I speak to Him Who knows all things, to Whom my whole inner life is manifest, and Who alone can perfectly comfort and help me.

You know what good things I am most in need of and how poor I am in virtue. Behold I stand before You, poor and naked, asking Your grace and imploring Your mercy.

Feed Your hungry beggar. Inflame my coldness with the fire of Your love. Enlighten my blindness with the brightness of Your presence. Turn all earthly things to bitterness for me, all grievance and adversity to patience, all lowly creation to contempt and oblivion. Raise my heart to You in heaven and suffer me not to wander on earth. From this moment to all eternity do You alone grow sweet to me, for You alone are my food and drink, my love and my joy, my sweetness and my total good.

Let Your presence wholly inflame me, consume and transform me into Yourself, that I may become one spirit with You by the grace of inward union and by the melting power of Your ardent love.

Suffer me not to go from You fasting and thirsty, but deal with me mercifully as You have so often and so wonderfully dealt with Your saints.

What wonder if I were completely inflamed by You to die to myself, since You are the fire ever burning and never dying, a love purifying the heart and enlightening the understanding.

The Seventeenth Chapter

THE BURNING LOVE AND STRONG DESIRE TO RECEIVE CHRIST

THE DISCIPLE

WITH GREATEST devotion and ardent love, with all affection and fervor of heart I wish to receive You, O Lord, as many saints and devout persons, most pleasing to You in their holiness of life and most fervent in devotion, desired You in Holy Communion.

O my God, everlasting love, my final good, my happiness unending, I long to receive You with as strong a desire and as worthy a reverence as any of the saints ever had or could have felt, and though I am not worthy to have all these sentiments of devotion, still I offer You the full affection of my heart as if I alone had all those most pleasing and ardent desires.

Yet, whatever a God-fearing mind can conceive and desire, I offer in its entirety to You with the greatest reverence and inward affection. I wish to keep nothing for self but to offer to You, willingly and most freely, myself and all that is mine.

O Lord God, my Creator and my Redeemer, I long to receive You this day with such reverence, praise, and honor, with such gratitude, worthiness and love, with such faith, hope, and purity as that with which Your most holy Mother, the glorious Virgin Mary, longed for and received You when she humbly and devoutly answered the angel who announced to her the mystery of the Incarnation: "Behold the handmaid of the Lord; be it done to me according to thy word."[1]

Likewise as Your blessed precursor, the most excellent of saints, John the Baptist, gladdened by Your presence, exulted in the Holy Ghost while yet enclosed in the womb of his mother, and afterward seeing Jesus walking among men, humbled himself and with devout love declared: "The friend of the bridegroom, who standeth and heareth him, rejoiceth with joy because of the bridegroom's voice,"[2] even so I long to be inflamed with great and holy desires and to give myself to You with all my heart.

Therefore I offer and present to You the gladness of all devout hearts, their ardent affection, their mental raptures, their supernatural illuminations and heavenly visions together with all the virtues and praises which have been or shall be celebrated by all creatures in heaven and on earth, for myself and all commended to my prayers, that You may be worthily praised and glorified forever.

Accept, O Lord my God, my promises and desires of giving You infinite praise and boundless benediction, which in the vastness of Your ineffable greatness are justly due You. This I render and desire to render every day and every moment of time, and in my loving prayers I invite and entreat all celestial spirits and all the faithful to join me in giving You praise and thanks.

Let all people, races, and tongues praise You and with the greatest joy and most ardent devotion magnify Your sweet and holy name. And let all who reverently and devoutly celebrate this most great Sacrament and receive it in the fullness of faith, find kindness and mercy in You and humbly pray for me, a sinner. And when they have received the longed-for devotion and blissful union, and, well consoled and wonderfully refreshed, have retired from Your holy, Your celestial table, may they deign to remember my poor soul.

The Eighteenth Chapter

MAN SHOULD NOT SCRUTINIZE THIS SACRAMENT IN CURIOSITY, BUT HUMBLY IMITATE CHRIST AND SUBMIT REASON TO HOLY FAITH

THE VOICE OF CHRIST

BEWARE OF curious and vain examination of this most profound Sacrament, if you do not wish to be plunged into the depths of doubt. He who scrutinizes its majesty too closely will be overwhelmed by its glory.

---

[1] Luke 1:38.
[2] John 3:29.

God can do more than man can understand. A pious and humble search for truth He will allow, a search that is ever ready to learn and that seeks to walk in the reasonable doctrine of the fathers.

Blest is the simplicity that leaves the difficult way of dispute and goes forward on the level, firm path of God's commandments. Many have lost devotion because they wished to search into things beyond them.

Faith is required of you, and a sincere life, not a lofty intellect nor a delving into the mysteries of God. If you neither know nor understand things beneath you, how can you comprehend what is above you? Submit yourself to God and humble reason to faith, and the light of understanding will be given you so far as it is good and necessary for you.

Some are gravely tempted concerning faith and the Sacrament but this disturbance is not laid to them but to the enemy.

Be not disturbed, dispute not in your mind, answer not the doubts sent by the devil, but believe the words of God, believe His saints and prophets and the evil enemy will flee from you. It is often very profitable for the servant of God to suffer such things. For Satan does not tempt unbelievers and sinners whom he already holds securely, but in many ways he does tempt and trouble the faithful servant.

Go forward, then, with sincere and unflinching faith, and with humble reverence approach this Sacrament. Whatever you cannot understand commit to the security of the all-powerful God, Who does not deceive you. The man, however, who trusts in himself is deceived. God walks with sincere men, reveals Himself to humble men, enlightens the understanding of pure minds, and hides His grace from the curious and the proud.

Human reason is weak and can be deceived. True faith, however, cannot be deceived. All reason and natural science ought to come after faith, not go before it, nor oppose it. For in this most holy and supremely excellent Sacrament, faith and love take precedence and work in a hidden manner.

God, eternal, incomprehensible, and infinitely powerful, does great and inscrutable things in heaven and on earth, and there is no searching into His marvelous works. If all the works of God were such that human reason could easily grasp them, they would not be called wonderful or beyond the power of words to tell.

POETRY

101 GREAT AMERICAN POEMS, Edited by The American Poetry & Literacy Project. (0-486-40158-8)

100 BEST-LOVED POEMS, Edited by Philip Smith. (0-486-28553-7)

ENGLISH ROMANTIC POETRY: An Anthology, Edited by Stanley Appelbaum. (0-486-29282-7)

THE INFERNO, Dante Alighieri. Translated and with notes by Henry Wadsworth Longfellow. (0-486-44288-8)

PARADISE LOST, John Milton. Introduction and Notes by John A. Himes. (0-486-44287-X)

SPOON RIVER ANTHOLOGY, Edgar Lee Masters. (0-486-27275-3)

SELECTED CANTERBURY TALES, Geoffrey Chaucer. (0-486-28241-4)

SELECTED POEMS, Emily Dickinson. (0-486-26466-1)

LEAVES OF GRASS: The Original 1855 Edition, Walt Whitman. (0-486-45676-5)

COMPLETE SONNETS, William Shakespeare. (0-486-26686-9)

THE RAVEN AND OTHER FAVORITE POEMS, Edgar Allan Poe. (0-486-26685-0)

ENGLISH VICTORIAN POETRY: An Anthology, Edited by Paul Negri. (0-486-40425-0)

SELECTED POEMS, Walt Whitman. (0-486-26878-0)

THE ROAD NOT TAKEN AND OTHER POEMS, Robert Frost. (0-486-27550-7)

AFRICAN-AMERICAN POETRY: An Anthology, 1773-1927, Edited by Joan R. Sherman. (0-486-29604-0)

GREAT SHORT POEMS, Edited by Paul Negri. (0-486-41105-2)

THE RIME OF THE ANCIENT MARINER, Samuel Taylor Coleridge. (0-486-27266-4)

THE WASTE LAND, PRUFROCK AND OTHER POEMS, T. S. Eliot. (0-486-40061-1)

SONG OF MYSELF, Walt Whitman. (0-486-41410-8)

AENEID, Vergil. (0-486-28749-1)

SONGS FOR THE OPEN ROAD: Poems of Travel and Adventure, Edited by The American Poetry & Literacy Project. (0-486-40646-6)

SONGS OF INNOCENCE AND SONGS OF EXPERIENCE, William Blake. (0-486-27051-3)

WORLD WAR ONE BRITISH POETS: Brooke, Owen, Sassoon, Rosenberg and Others, Edited by Candace Ward. (0-486-29568-0)

GREAT SONNETS, Edited by Paul Negri. (0-486-28052-7)

CHRISTMAS CAROLS: Complete Verses, Edited by Shane Weller. (0-486-27397-0)

POETRY

GREAT POEMS BY AMERICAN WOMEN: An Anthology, Edited by Susan L. Rattiner. (0-486-40164-2)

FAVORITE POEMS, Henry Wadsworth Longfellow. (0-486-27273-7)

BHAGAVADGITA, Translated by Sir Edwin Arnold. (0-486-27782-8)

ESSAY ON MAN AND OTHER POEMS, Alexander Pope. (0-486-28053-5)

GREAT LOVE POEMS, Edited by Shane Weller. (0-486-27284-2)

DOVER BEACH AND OTHER POEMS, Matthew Arnold. (0-486-28037-3)

THE SHOOTING OF DAN MCGREW AND OTHER POEMS, Robert Service. (0-486-27556-6)

THE BALLAD OF READING GAOL AND OTHER POEMS, Oscar Wilde. (0-486-27072-6)

SELECTED POEMS OF RUMI, Jalalu'l-Din Rumi. (0-486-41583-X)

SELECTED POEMS OF GERARD MANLEY HOPKINS, Gerard Manley Hopkins. Edited and with an Introduction by Bob Blaisdell. (0-486-47867-X)

RENASCENCE AND OTHER POEMS, Edna St. Vincent Millay. (0-486-26873-X)

THE RUBÁIYÁT OF OMAR KHAYYÁM: First and Fifth Editions, Edward FitzGerald. (0-486-26467-X)

TO MY HUSBAND AND OTHER POEMS, Anne Bradstreet. (0-486-41408-6)

LITTLE ORPHANT ANNIE AND OTHER POEMS, James Whitcomb Riley. (0-486-28260-0)

IMAGIST POETRY: AN ANTHOLOGY, Edited by Bob Blaisdell. (0-486-40875-2)

FIRST FIG AND OTHER POEMS, Edna St. Vincent Millay. (0-486-41104-4)

GREAT SHORT POEMS FROM ANTIQUITY TO THE TWENTIETH CENTURY, Edited by Dorothy Belle Pollack. (0-486-47876-9)

THE FLOWERS OF EVIL & PARIS SPLEEN: Selected Poems, Charles Baudelaire. Translated by Wallace Fowlie. (0-486-47545-X)

CIVIL WAR SHORT STORIES AND POEMS, Edited by Bob Blaisdell. (0-486-48226-X)

EARLY POEMS, Edna St. Vincent Millay. (0-486-43672-1)

JABBERWOCKY AND OTHER POEMS, Lewis Carroll. (0-486-41582-1)

THE METAMORPHOSES: Selected Stories in Verse, Ovid. (0-486-42758-7)

IDYLLS OF THE KING, Alfred, Lord Tennyson. Edited by W. J. Rolfe. (0-486-43795-7)

A BOY'S WILL AND NORTH OF BOSTON, Robert Frost. (0-486-26866-7)

100 FAVORITE ENGLISH AND IRISH POEMS, Edited by Clarence C. Strowbridge. (0-486-44429-5)

FICTION

FLATLAND: A ROMANCE OF MANY DIMENSIONS, Edwin A. Abbott. (0-486-27263-X)

PRIDE AND PREJUDICE, Jane Austen. (0-486-28473-5)

CIVIL WAR SHORT STORIES AND POEMS, Edited by Bob Blaisdell. (0-486-48226-X)

THE DECAMERON: Selected Tales, Giovanni Boccaccio. Edited by Bob Blaisdell. (0-486-41113-3)

JANE EYRE, Charlotte Brontë. (0-486-42449-9)

WUTHERING HEIGHTS, Emily Brontë. (0-486-29256-8)

THE THIRTY-NINE STEPS, John Buchan. (0-486-28201-5)

ALICE'S ADVENTURES IN WONDERLAND, Lewis Carroll. (0-486-27543-4)

MY ÁNTONIA, Willa Cather. (0-486-28240-6)

THE AWAKENING, Kate Chopin. (0-486-27786-0)

HEART OF DARKNESS, Joseph Conrad. (0-486-26464-5)

LORD JIM, Joseph Conrad. (0-486-40650-4)

THE RED BADGE OF COURAGE, Stephen Crane. (0-486-26465-3)

THE WORLD'S GREATEST SHORT STORIES, Edited by James Daley. (0-486-44716-2)

A CHRISTMAS CAROL, Charles Dickens. (0-486-26865-9)

GREAT EXPECTATIONS, Charles Dickens. (0-486-41586-4)

A TALE OF TWO CITIES, Charles Dickens. (0-486-40651-2)

CRIME AND PUNISHMENT, Fyodor Dostoyevsky. Translated by Constance Garnett. (0-486-41587-2)

THE ADVENTURES OF SHERLOCK HOLMES, Sir Arthur Conan Doyle. (0-486-47491-7)

THE HOUND OF THE BASKERVILLES, Sir Arthur Conan Doyle. (0-486-28214-7)

BLAKE: PROPHET AGAINST EMPIRE, David V. Erdman. (0-486-26719-9)

WHERE ANGELS FEAR TO TREAD, E. M. Forster. (0-486-27791-7)

BEOWULF, Translated by R. K. Gordon. (0-486-27264-8)

THE RETURN OF THE NATIVE, Thomas Hardy. (0-486-43165-7)

THE SCARLET LETTER, Nathaniel Hawthorne. (0-486-28048-9)

SIDDHARTHA, Hermann Hesse. (0-486-40653-9)

THE ODYSSEY, Homer. (0-486-40654-7)

THE TURN OF THE SCREW, Henry James. (0-486-26684-2)

DUBLINERS, James Joyce. (0-486-26870-5)

FICTION

THE METAMORPHOSIS AND OTHER STORIES, Franz Kafka. (0-486-29030-1)

SONS AND LOVERS, D. H. Lawrence. (0-486-42121-X)

THE CALL OF THE WILD, Jack London. (0-486-26472-6)

GREAT AMERICAN SHORT STORIES, Edited by Paul Negri. (0-486-42119-8)

THE GOLD-BUG AND OTHER TALES, Edgar Allan Poe. (0-486-26875-6)

ANTHEM, Ayn Rand. (0-486-49277-X)

FRANKENSTEIN, Mary Shelley. (0-486-28211-2)

THE JUNGLE, Upton Sinclair. (0-486-41923-1)

THREE LIVES, Gertrude Stein. (0-486-28059-4)

THE STRANGE CASE OF DR. JEKYLL AND MR. HYDE, Robert Louis Stevenson. (0-486-26688-5)

DRACULA, Bram Stoker. (0-486-41109-5)

UNCLE TOM'S CABIN, Harriet Beecher Stowe. (0-486-44028-1)

ADVENTURES OF HUCKLEBERRY FINN, Mark Twain. (0-486-28061-6)

THE ADVENTURES OF TOM SAWYER, Mark Twain. (0-486-40077-8)

CANDIDE, Voltaire. Edited by Francois-Marie Arouet. (0-486-26689-3)

THE COUNTRY OF THE BLIND: and Other Science-Fiction Stories, H. G. Wells. Edited by Martin Gardner. (0-486-48289-8)

THE WAR OF THE WORLDS, H. G. Wells. (0-486-29506-0)

ETHAN FROME, Edith Wharton. (0-486-26690-7)

THE PICTURE OF DORIAN GRAY, Oscar Wilde. (0-486-27807-7)

MONDAY OR TUESDAY: Eight Stories, Virginia Woolf. (0-486-29453-6)

NONFICTION

POETICS, Aristotle. (0-486-29577-X)

MEDITATIONS, Marcus Aurelius. (0-486-29823-X)

THE WAY OF PERFECTION, St. Teresa of Avila. Edited and Translated by E. Allison Peers. (0-486-48451-3)

THE DEVIL'S DICTIONARY, Ambrose Bierce. (0-486-27542-6)

GREAT SPEECHES OF THE 20TH CENTURY, Edited by Bob Blaisdell. (0-486-47467-4)

THE COMMUNIST MANIFESTO AND OTHER REVOLUTIONARY WRITINGS: Marx, Marat, Paine, Mao Tse-Tung, Gandhi and Others, Edited by Bob Blaisdell. (0-486-42465-0)

INFAMOUS SPEECHES: From Robespierre to Osama bin Laden, Edited by Bob Blaisdell. (0-486-47849-1)

GREAT ENGLISH ESSAYS: From Bacon to Chesterton, Edited by Bob Blaisdell. (0-486-44082-6)

GREEK AND ROMAN ORATORY, Edited by Bob Blaisdell. (0-486-49622-8)

THE UNITED STATES CONSTITUTION: The Full Text with Supplementary Materials, Edited and with supplementary materials by Bob Blaisdell. (0-486-47166-7)

GREAT SPEECHES BY NATIVE AMERICANS, Edited by Bob Blaisdell. (0-486-41122-2)

GREAT SPEECHES BY AFRICAN AMERICANS: Frederick Douglass, Sojourner Truth, Dr. Martin Luther King, Jr., Barack Obama, and Others, Edited by James Daley. (0-486-44761-8)

GREAT SPEECHES BY AMERICAN WOMEN, Edited by James Daley. (0-486-46141-6)

HISTORY'S GREATEST SPEECHES, Edited by James Daley. (0-486-49739-9)

GREAT INAUGURAL ADDRESSES, Edited by James Daley. (0-486-44577-1)

GREAT SPEECHES ON GAY RIGHTS, Edited by James Daley. (0-486-47512-3)

ON THE ORIGIN OF SPECIES: By Means of Natural Selection, Charles Darwin. (0-486-45006-6)

NARRATIVE OF THE LIFE OF FREDERICK DOUGLASS, Frederick Douglass. (0-486-28499-9)

THE SOULS OF BLACK FOLK, W. E. B. Du Bois. (0-486-28041-1)

NATURE AND OTHER ESSAYS, Ralph Waldo Emerson. (0-486-46947-6)

SELF-RELIANCE AND OTHER ESSAYS, Ralph Waldo Emerson. (0-486-27790-9)

THE LIFE OF OLAUDAH EQUIANO, Olaudah Equiano. (0-486-40661-X)

WIT AND WISDOM FROM POOR RICHARD'S ALMANACK, Benjamin Franklin. (0-486-40891-4)

THE AUTOBIOGRAPHY OF BENJAMIN FRANKLIN, Benjamin Franklin. (0-486-29073-5)